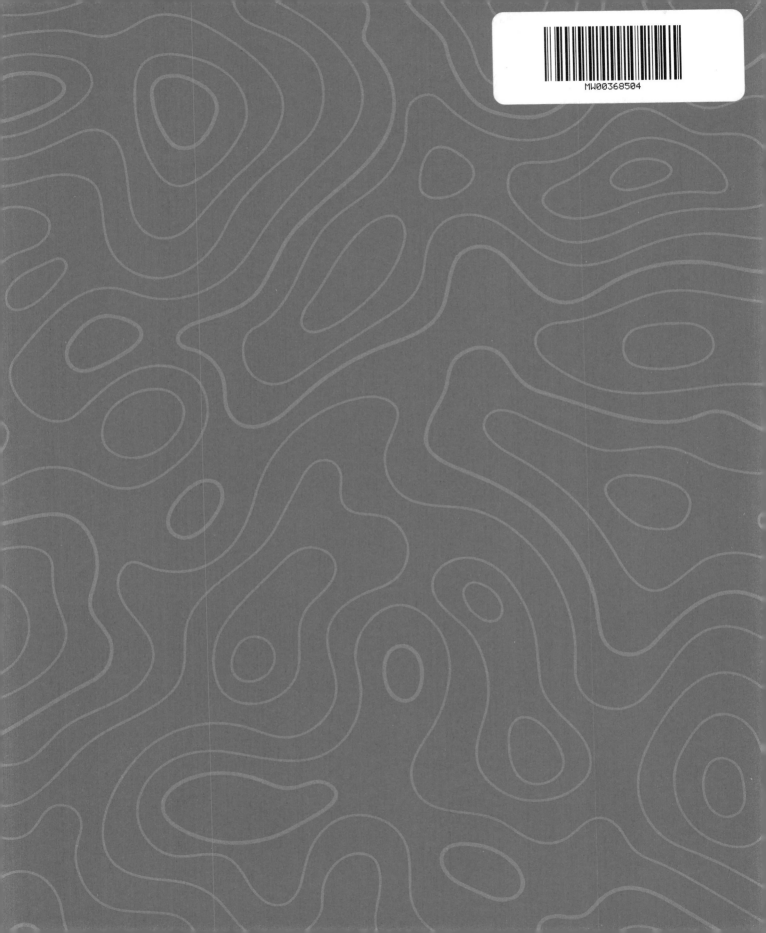

States *of* Adventure

States *of* *Adventure*

30 outdoor adventure stories about
finding yourself by getting lost

Fitz Cahall
host of
The Dirtbag
Diaries

Contents

Foreword

In the winter of 2006 I got dropped off in the Pit—a cheap campground outside of Bishop, California—the day after a heavy blizzard had blanketed the region in several feet of snow. Most climbers had fled the storm, but I was committed—I pitched my three-season backpacking tent in the dry footprint of a less intrepid camper's abandoned campsite. My old minivan had just given up and died, so I settled in for a very cold winter in my tent with my bicycle. I didn't own a stove or real camping gear, but I biked to the crag or boulders every day and climbed my heart out all season.

Fitz Cahall launched the *Dirtbag Diaries* podcast at roughly the same time that I was starting to cut my teeth as a dirtbag climber. He'd been living on the road, trying to make it as an outdoor journalist, when he realized that he could reach a much broader audience through the Internet. The podcast has flourished for more than 17 years because Fitz has a talent for unearthing beautiful, honest stories from the outdoors and making them relatable.

This comes naturally to Fitz because he is, in many ways, the definition of an everyman climber. He's good enough to get outside and have big adventures in the mountains, but he would never lose sight of his other commitments in the process. He balances his own outdoor pursuits with those of his wife and two sons, supporting their endeavors while still maintaining his lifelong career in the outdoor industry. He is someone to look up to; a dirtbag who "made it." In many ways his life mirrors an episode of the *Dirtbag Diaries*.

This makes Fitz the perfect author for *States of Adventure*, sharing the very best stories from his years at the helm of the *Dirtbag Diaries*. The stories are incredibly varied—they range from kayaking the Grand Canyon to paragliding the length of the Canadian Rockies to trail magic on the Appalachian Trail. But they are universally moving. You will find each one both touching and inspiring—the kinds of stories that can make you both misty-eyed and antsy to get outside.

One of the common threads throughout the book is that anyone can find their true self—and generally their best self—while challenging themselves outdoors. As Fitz states in the introduction, "Who you are in the mountains is who you are." I was certainly shaped by that cold, car-less winter in Bishop, and my many outdoor adventures since. I'm sure that your adventures will do the same.

So enjoy the book, then go outside.

Alex Honnold

THIS PAGE Alex climbs *Passage to Freedom* on El Capitan in Yosemite Valley.

Introduction
Three Ways to Have Fun

FITZ CAHALL

RIGHT Snowboarding in fresh powder is pure Type I fun.

My children hate coffee, which given their age is a good thing. Actually, hate probably isn't the right word. Coffee puzzles them. Coffee sparks a visceral curiosity. When Dad takes a sip, they witness a look of contentment or hope for the day, or a flickering of imagination slide across his face. When they try it, they taste what could only be described as the remnants of a high school chemistry experiment gone terribly wrong. The bitter liquid burns. The acidity gathers on the back of their tongues. The sputtering and coughing start just before they lurch away with disgust not just at the coffee overwhelming their taste buds, but also the realization that they're directly descended from this crustacean of questionable judgment and palette.

But I notice that through the years they keep stealing sips. They seem vaguely aware that in the years to come it is they who will change rather than the flavor of coffee. That their own binary understanding of what is enjoyable may not be static.

FUN, TOO, HAS FLAVORS

Type I fun. It sounds like it's going to be fun. It's enjoyable in the moment. In hindsight, it's a blast. You'd recommend it to a friend, 10 out of 10. It includes, but is not limited to: climbing crisp granite edges in the soft warmth of the October sun; floating effortlessly through 18in (46cm) of newly fallen January snow; and the great conversation around the campfire following a long day

RIGHT There are times in any adventure when the definition of fun begins to stretch.

paddling rivers fed by spring snowmelt. It is that feeling from childhood of careering down the block on your first bicycle or the shriek of cold water pouring from the garden hose on a hot summer day. The majority of time spent outdoors falls into this category.

Type II fun is where the fun begins to evolve. The flavor becomes more complex. Type II fun often sounds like it's going to be fun, but during the day's adventure, the definition of fun begins to stretch. This type of fun often begins or ends in the dark. After hours of effort, practitioners of Type II fun report relief when said activity ends, although they are not quite tired enough to admit it publicly. It is a weekend backpacking trip, compressed into a single long day. Winter camping deep inside snowy ranges. Bushwhacks to unforgettable alpine vistas. Side effects include blisters, scratches, and the occasional bruised ego. You will exert past the point of comfort and confront the reality that a misstep in the wrong place will come with consequences. Fears are confronted. Wrong turns righted. Self-imposed boundaries successfully challenged. Stories made. Type II fun is a place of learning, where skill sets solidify, horizons expand, and confidence bubbles up like a spring at the mountain's base. Because of thirst, Type II fun is always a blast to talk about over a beer at the pub.

AND THEN, TYPE III FUN

In the planning stages, it doesn't sound like fun. There are hazards to be mitigated. Hard conversations about risk to be had. The gear list dwindles to just the necessities, and comfort is always left behind. The execution confirms the hypothesis—this idea turned current predicament is indeed no fun. The cold settles deep into the bone, enough so that it might induce a phenomena dubbed "The Screaming Barfies," where the rush of blood into overly cold limbs induces a pain which either makes the hapless adventurer scream or vomit, or maybe both simultaneously. A Type III adventure may potentially involve megafauna. Remember, one way to survive a bear attack is to run faster than your partner. Jokes aside, Type III guarantees discomfort, fear, and a slow erosion of ego until the barriers between a person and the natural world become so thin as to almost vanish. Congratulations, you are now a part of the ecosystem.

But a curious thing happens once the adventure is endured or survived. Chris Darwin, conservationist, climber, and great-great-grandson of Charles Darwin, summed up the paradox of Type III fun the best when he said, "Climbing at altitude is like hitting your head against a brick wall—it's great when you stop."

Inside these pages we hope you see a version of yourself, no matter what leg of the journey through life you currently inhabit.

Shards of memories glow like embers, growing into a blaze that sustains profound feelings of gratitude, friendship or catharsis. It turns out the stars burn brightest at 3am. Difficult endeavors contain meaning. Who you are in the mountains is who you are. Type III fun has a way of revealing those truths.

While that sort of deep self-reflection can be attained in other ways, the stillness that comes from the grandest adventures has a unique flavor, one that some of us grow to savor. One thing is for certain – Type III fun makes for the best stories. This has been the bread and butter of this podcasting experiment we call the *Dirtbag Diaries*.

So often we get the question: "What makes a dirtbag?" Most think of the young 20-something men and women frozen in iconic 1970s climbing photos. They scraped by on cafeteria leftovers gleaned from the plates of tourists in Yosemite Valley while in pursuit of the climbing craft. A means to an end. It's a romantic, "stick it the man," bohemian ideal from a different decade, and it's mostly make-believe these days. To outsiders, they were hedonistic slackers, but those on the inside understood they were chasing a physical art form and building powerful life connections in the process.

The dirtbag spirit of those early Yosemite climbers—do more with less—has evolved through the decades, becoming a cultural movement producing offshoots like #VanLife or "Tiny Homes." It hinges around a few simple questions.

To lead lives of meaning, should we collect the latest and greatest stuff? Or should we spend it with people we love in places that fill us with wonder? To find purpose, should we seek out corporate ladders? Or build powerful connections in order to build powerful communities organized around mindset rather than geography? What can we let go of in order to find a better balance between personal passion and the wonderful responsibilities to family, community and the planet?

The stories contained here are the work of those who have collaboratively shepherded the *Dirtbag Diaries* podcast through the last two decades alongside me—Jen Altschul, Cordelia Zars, Ashlee Langholz and Becca Cahall. This show thrived when it grew past my own voice. Inside these pages we hope you see a version of yourself, no matter what leg of the journey through life you currently inhabit. Maybe you're about to take those first magical steps into the outdoor life. Or you've built your skills and are looking for new ideas or challenges. Perhaps, as it is for me, you find yourself in the din of middle age, juggling to keep the quiet of natural spaces a part of my own and my family's life. Some of you will be returning to a simpler time, with more free hours and happy to move at a confident, but unrushed pace.

Go. Explore. Adventure. Return changed.

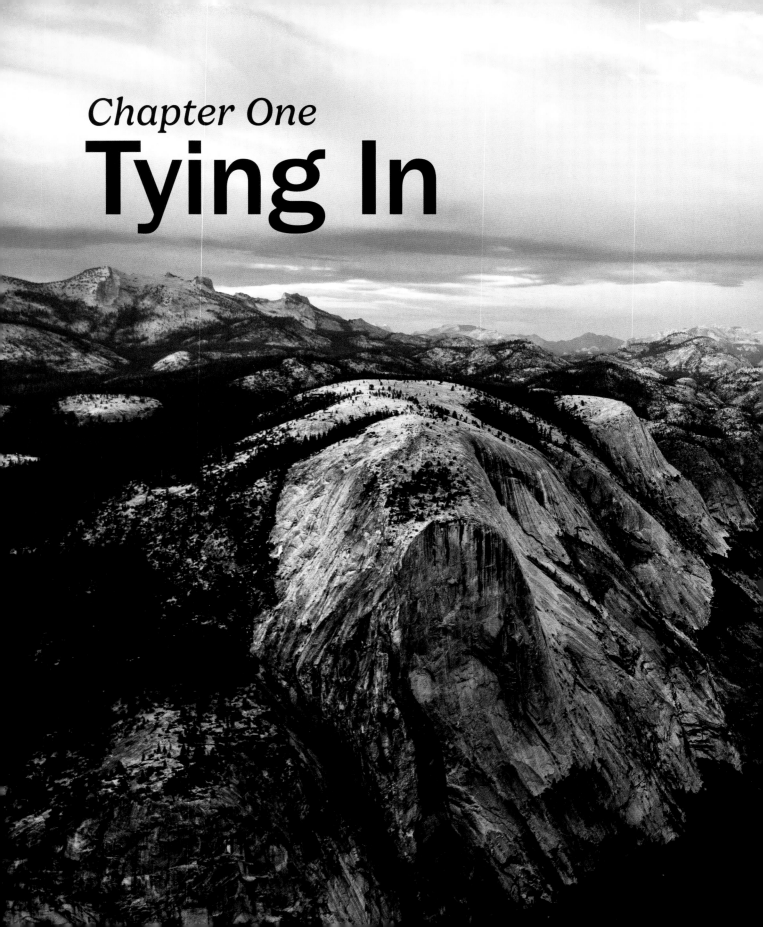

Chapter One
Tying In

THE MONOBOARD

LOCATION	**LAKE TAHOE, CA**
PEOPLE	**LANDLORD HENRY**
ACTIVITY	**MONOBOARDING, SKIING**

ABOVE Monoboards originated in the 1950s but never gained the same foothold as snowboarding.

The
Monoboard

FITZ CAHALL

After two months of looking for a place to rent for the winter in Tahoe, we finally had a lead that didn't include single-pane windows or thin insulation. Becca and I were a little concerned about living directly beneath our landlord. We weren't prone to partying or intensely private, but oft-seen landlords—especially wealthy ones who weekend where you live—can be a pain. The rent for our 150 sq-ft basement studio was fair and the view unbeatable. Lake Tahoe lapped against toaster-sized stones just a hundred feet from our patio. It was the first, and probably last, lakefront property we'd call home.

FIRST IMPRESSIONS

I was still having doubts when we pulled into the driveway to meet our new landlord, but after two months of couch-surfing we were getting desperate for a place of our own.

"Honey, we ski. Some people buy second homes. We all have different hobbies. It will work out," Becca told me.

I stared at the three-story, lakefront home that we'd play guard over from the tiny room adjacent to the garage.

"They'll probably never even come up," I said. "Real estate is just the thing to do these days."

We don't like to admit it, but mountain people can be an arrogant lot. We adhere to an "us and them" view of the world. To those we deem insufficiently faithful to a life shaped around the pursuit of the next powder day or sun-kissed granite walls, we save our greatest insults. *Gaper. Kook. Jerry. Gumbie. Weekend Warrior.*

As we met Henry to exchange the first and last month's rent for keys, I immediately placed him outside the circle of true-believers. Small in stature with wiry, graying hair, and a quiet voice that tended to jump and skip through sentences like the trebling of a distant bird call, Henry worked in the Bay Area as a labor lawyer.

As he clicked the garage door opener, the only means of access to the studio, both Becca and I immediately trained our gaze to the farthest wall as the mechanical door slid upward, spilling light into the garage. We blinked in awe, which was probably Henry's intention.

The garage smelled faintly of laundry detergent, old paint, and motor oil. And there, in front of us, lay Henry's true life's work.

A KINDRED SPIRIT

It was immediately clear Henry had searched yard sales and cut-rate ski shops unloading aging rental fleets. He'd responded to newspaper advertisements and helped neighbors clean out their garages in order to assemble what was likely the most extensive collection of rare, bizarre, and antique skis in the West. This was not a museum where antiquities were kept behind glass and never used—but a working library where items were checked out and returned with scratches, dings, and delaminated side walls.

There were at least 10 pairs of skis hanging from a homemade wooden rack. For early season, sparse conditions, Henry kept two battered sets—each with their own unique gashes and core shots. Next to them, hung an old pair of straight skis Henry kept for "shits and giggles."

"I dust them off every once and a while just to remember the old days," he told me.

He owned a newer pair of Dynastars, nothing flashy, just a good workhorse of a ski and two other pairs that he kept around. He also had an original pair of fat powder skis complete with neon surveyor's tape, in case of a wipe out. Of all the skis in his collection, they were the only set purchased new—something that made Henry startlingly ahead of the curve.

There were snowboards. Short boards for the park. Long for the powder. He admitted that snow blades had disappointed him as they didn't do anything well.

He pointed to two sets of 1980s beginner skis, cut short in the rear to facilitate wedge turns.

"These," Henry said with an eager smile and look of conspiratorial joy, "are perfect for doing spread eagles and daffys."

I struggled to imagine this small, quiet man with a neatly trimmed mustache and wire-rimmed glasses ripping the shit out of anything other than a legal brief, but the collection showed that our unassuming landlord knew a thing or two about carving a turn. At the very least, this man could have fun with a couple of two-by-fours strapped to his feet.

And then. Like a star at the center of a galaxy, sat a blue, white, red, and gold monoboard.

"It's awesome," Henry whispered in reverence. I searched for any hint of irony. There wasn't any. "It's best on groomer days but only after lunch and a few beers," Henry said, looking at me as if to size me up. "You've got to ride at the end of the day, because after you strap that bad boy on you can't remember how to turn a ski or a snowboard," he continued, as if that were a selling point. He rounded out his collection with cross-country skis, three saucers, a wooden toboggan, and tri-ski complete with steering wheel.

A MAN APART

People have been skiing for centuries, and while side cuts, dampening systems, shapes, and bindings have advanced light years, the heart of the sport remains rooted in a simple truth—sliding on snow is fun. A gifted carpenter understands each tool in his box. Henry understood each ski, each snowboard's wild breed of goofy fun. He did it with a lightness unencumbered by worries of how a 50-year-old man on snow blades might be judged. Standing in that garage, I understood immediately that Henry was every bit a part of the community as me.

I'm sure punk snowboarders snickered at Henry's monoboard. I'm sure mocking cheers floated down from the lifts when Henry, employing his hybrid beginner skis, punctuated yet another successful daffy with a quiet whoop of joy. If Henry heard the remarks, I'm sure he didn't care. The smile on his face would last for at least a week as he herded briefs and culled depositions into neatly arranged cases.

One January Friday, Becca and I returned late to find a recently arrived Henry with shovel in hand, standing in

"You've got to ride at the end of the day, because after you strap that bad boy on you can't remember how to turn a ski or a snowboard," he continued, as if that were a selling point.

the driveway and illuminated by the porch light. When I reminded Henry that he had hired a vastly efficient, six-ton plow to complete the task for the entire winter and it would be along shortly, he just smiled giddily and said: "I know, but it just looked like it needed to be shoveled." With a smile, he went back to work and Becca and I joined in as the snow fell in thick wet flakes.

HOME IS WHERE YOU MAKE IT

It's been years since I've seen Henry. Now, I live farther from the windswept ridgelines and water-carved canyons than I have in more than a decade. Sometimes in dreams, I hear the rasp of a snow shovel's metal edge on snow-slicked concrete. Both Becca and I long for that tiny studio with the trundle bed and the incredible view. We followed our careers out of the mountains, and now understand the motivation that it takes to negotiate rainy interstates, chain controlled passes, and the vehicular chaos that comes with transporting yourself to your playground. While I live in the lowlands, it doesn't make me any less of a mountain person. I know that one day I will become the subject of young snowboarders' ridicule and the lifties will mutter "city folk" under their breath. I hope I will find solace in half-shoveled driveways and snow falling in thick round flakes.

Now, when I descend into the red glare of brake lights on the road back toward another week of work in the city's windy, concrete slot canyons, I think of Henry illuminated by my headlights—shovel in hand, snowflakes melting on the edges of his mustache, smiling like an expat returning to a homeland after decades abroad.

At the very least, this man could have fun with a couple of two-by-fours strapped to his feet.

THIS PAGE Patience pays off when waiting for a bluebird powder day.

WINNEBAGO WARRIORS

📍 LOCATIONS   **LEES FERRY TO PEARCE FERRY, COLORADO RIVER**

PEOPLE   **THE HOLCOMBE FAMILY**

ACTIVITY   **KAYAKING**

ABOVE 13-year-old Abby Holcombe is ready to launch.

Winnebago
Warriors

FITZ CAHALL

The menacing roar of millions of gallons of water churning over stone made it hard to think, let alone have a conversation. The chaos of infinite water molecules colliding and carving bedrock reverberated in Abby Holcombe's chest. The Grand Canyon—with its astonishing relief and furrowed temples of sandstone turrets and ridges—produces the feeling of smallness in those who visit, and Abby stood perched on perhaps the most humbling locale in the world.

"I really want to run it. It's really big. So big it's making me nauseous, but I really want to run it," Abby said into the camera.

Behind her, the Colorado River continued its erosive assault of the canyon through the rapid known as Lava Falls. Eons ago, a large lava flow slid down the red sandstone walls, pinching the Colorado River into a tight channel of whitewater. The river's famed muddy

red waters pour into a series of ever-increasing waves, cresting so high they fall backward on themselves. The river's strength is enough to twist and bend metal.

Abby continued, "I feel like if I don't run it, it will be unfinished business. And I'm not sure I'll be able to get on another trip right away after this, since it took so long for my parents to get this one trip."

Standing on the edge of a dream always requires one last moment of commitment. Most people who venture down the Grand Canyon do so via the relative safety of the massive, commercial whitewater rafts, steered by seasoned guides and often assisted by motors. Still, Lava Falls occasionally tosses, flips, and scatters the contents of the rafts, people included. Occasionally, it claims lives. To navigate the river in a kayak requires an alchemy of athleticism and boldness. Only the most seasoned kayakers drop into Lava. Desperately close to achieving a complete kayaking descent of the Grand Canyon—linking its 80 named rapids without portaging or swimming—Abby faced the last truly difficult hurdle.

Moments like these present an opportunity to walk right up to our fears, pick them apart, and then try to reassemble them into purpose. But no 12-year-old delivers themselves to a defining life moment without having seen their parents do the same.

TAKING THE PLUNGE

Three years earlier, Abby watched her parents, Kathy and Peter, calculate their own incredible leap into a different way of living. After years of casually discussing the idea of taking their family on the road to climb, kayak, and explore the US, the couple put their Boulder, CO, house up for sale. It sold within three hours. Firmly in the current of their decision, the next week Peter bought an RV in Texas, before the family sold the majority of their possessions and packed the remainder into their new home on wheels.

"We'd always talked about it. We'd always dreamed about it," says Kathy. "I didn't want to get old and fade away, wondering if that was something that could have changed everything for us. I hoped Abby would see Peter and I chasing our dreams."

The Holcombes, both photojournalists, traveled regularly for work, and their jobs were geographically flexible. Abby signed up for online school for the fundamentals, but the American West and its rivers became her classroom as the family followed good weather to kayak and climb. As she navigated rivers, she learned about watersheds and saw the impacts of pollution and dams. Geology became tangible on hikes in Arches National Park. The history of the California Gold Rush came to life when Abby found glimmering flecks of the precious metal in the American River. She learned about volcanoes and glaciers by exploring Mount Rainier in Washington. They watched Alaskan grizzly bears from the window of their RV. Abby captained an 80-ft schooner in the Gulf of Mexico. She began competing in freestyle kayaking events the way most kids sign up for soccer and became a national champion (and on her way to an eventual world championship). The family thrived.

GRAND AMBITIONS
Yet, years later, Kathy still used the word "nightmare" to describe those initial moments of selling the house and downsizing their lives. The Holcombes stood safely on top of a rapid; downstream they could see the desired outcome. Between lay the chaos of lateral waves and uncertainty. In these moments, it feels exceedingly difficult to know whether you've made a good or bad decision, which is why most people simply don't make either choice.

That third year on the road, Peter and Kathy entered the annual lottery for a Grand Canyon River permit after seven years of striking out. To preserve the delicate river bottom landscape, wildlife, and the natural experience of boaters, the National Park Service (NPS) regulates the number of rafting parties that launch in a day. For a private group hoping to navigate the river without the benefit of a commercially guided trip, the Colorado River's lottery is the most sought after and the most difficult to get. The Holcombes hit the jackpot. They assembled a small group of friends with decades of river and guiding experience. Most of the team—Abby, Peter and Kathy—would be in kayaks but a few would be in rafts. Abby had paddled another classic river, the Main Fork of the Salmon in Idaho, and managed to kayak all the rapids. Could she do the same on the Grand?

THE RIVER WILD
Every Grand Canyon trip begins at Lees Ferry, where the Colorado pours cold, clear, and calm from the bottom of Lake Powell and the Glen Canyon Dam. Most whitewater is rated on a simple Class I–V system.

The Colorado earns its own rating system of 1–10. The consequences or technicality aren't necessarily greater than other rivers, but that much water creates bigger waves and holes. After all, these are the forces that carved the Grand Canyon.

At mile 17, the river began to flex its muscles. Alongside her father, Abby darted the tiny pink boat she'd become famous for into House Rock Rapid. The Roaring Twenties gave the boaters a taste of what's to come with 10 miles of nearly continuous whitewater as the river bed narrows or steepens, forming wave trains as the water moves downstream. In river parlance, parties navigate and avoid keeper holes, a vortex of recycling water capable of flipping rafts and sweeping their passengers downstream. Careful scouting from the river's banks revealed pathways through the hydrology. Still, a plan is just a plan until a boater paddles in. Through that first week, the rapids got no bigger than class 6. In between the chaos, Abby bobbed along the more tranquil sections of flatwater in her kayak. At night, the family would make camp inside the great cathedral of the canyon, Abby assembling and taking down her tent each day. Large sandy beaches made for perfect campsites as the stars burned brightly in one of the country's darkest patches of night sky. A trip like this is a potent cocktail of heightened focus and deep calm. Most just call it life-changing.

At mile 77, the rapids start getting bigger. Hance Rapid demands attention, followed 13 miles later by Horn Rapid. Abby breezed through them. At mile 94, she encountered Granite Rapid, a class 8.

"That was the first time on the trip that I'd seen fear in her eyes," remembered Peter. "You get your first glimpse of this rapid and it's just giant, churning with holes the size of Greyhound buses. Obviously, I'm there as a parent and I can say yes or no if I don't feel good about it, but I wanted to hear her work it out on her own."

Abby picked her line, but as she dropped into Granite she thought, "Oh my gosh, what did I get myself into?"

On the second wave, Abby flipped—her kayak upside down in the torrent of muddy water. At that moment, kayakers have two choices: roll or swim. "This," Peter immediately thought, "is a horrible place to swim." With the speed of a seasoned veteran and caring parent, Peter's mind fired through scenarios that might unfold in the coming seconds. If she pulled out of the boat, the PFD, a whitewater specific life vest, would hopefully pull her to the surface, but hydraulics in these rapids were big enough to pull a boat down to the river's bottom. He needed to be ready to grab her at the bottom of the rapid if she swam.

Then, Abby rolled her kayak, popping her head above the water. Peter exhaled and then watched as the next wave tossed her upside down once again.

"This is a big pounding," remembers Abby. "It just felt like my boat almost sank." Running out of air, she tried to roll once more. Seconds ticked by as she struggled to engage her roll and then she was upright, through Granite and paddling toward Peter in the eddy.

Abby kept stepping up to the challenge. Just after Granite, she successfully ran Hermit, which may be the second most difficult rapid in the Canyon. For 100 miles, Peter observed Abby paddle and strive with grace. They had scouted the big rapids, assessing the best lines, and talking through the possible outcomes. Abby found herself to be in the perfect position to cleanly paddle the entire descent, but one massive test of courage, technique, and will remained —Lava Falls.

Lava checks in at class 10. The biggest. The baddest. It's famed for claiming boats and is permanently affixed in American whitewater lore. Here, the river drops precipitously and with increasing speed. Lava is so big that it contains named features inside the rapid. Ledge Hole haunts the upper portion. To river right, V crests high and then slams into the Big Kahuna waves. Avoid Avocado Rock at all costs. To river left, Son of Lava Rapid awaits those who miss the safety of the river right eddy. Complete the maelstrom and most parties regroup and calm their nerves at the deservedly named Tequila Beach.

Peter watched his daughter from a distance, giving her space to make her own decisions. Abby paced back and forth on the shore for an hour, adjusting to the sheer size of the rapid and finding a line in her mind. "She came up to me and said, 'Okay, I know where I want to run it. Let's go. Let's go right now,'" remembers Peter.

Together, they pushed their boats into the river. Peter led the way toward the horizon line. Abby watched as he accelerated and disappeared out of view into the tumult. The river pulled her in. Each wave formed its own deep canyon. The kayaks accelerated down the backside of the wave. The speed of each descending wave pulled on their stomachs like a roller-coaster ride. Then up, up, up toward the wave crest and where it momentarily felt like

the river might slingshot them into the sky. Down again through "Big Kahuna's." Peter flipped. Rolled back up and looked for his daughter. Rising to the top of the next wave, he glimpsed Abby and her little pink boat perfectly on line, searching for the safety of the eddy where they could collect their breath and celebrate.

"I ran Lava clean. I didn't flip," Abby exclaimed. The remaining rapids, while still difficult and deserving respect, would all seem easier compared to what she'd just achieved.

When the Holcombes pulled out at Pearce Ferry a week later, Abby had accomplished the exceptional feat of a complete kayaking descent of the Grand Canyon. It wouldn't make her rich. It wouldn't make her famous. She would get a well-deserved ice cream. And while the NPS doesn't keep track of its oldest or youngest paddlers, what they can say is that Abby's 5'2" pink kayak was the smallest boat ever paddled from Lees Ferry to Pearce Ferry without a swim or a portage.

Adapted from reporting by Jen Altschul

PAGE 28 The Holcombes gathered together a highly experienced team of friends to help facilitate Abby's journey.

RIGHT Abby successfully completes another one of 80 sections of rapids, which at their most challenging are given a difficulty rating of class 10.

The speed of each descending wave pulled on their stomachs like a roller-coaster ride. Then up, up, up toward the wave crest and where it momentarily felt like the river might slingshot them into the sky.

ZARSIAN ADVENTURES

📍 LOCATION	**ELKHEAD VALLEY, CO**	
PEOPLE	**CORDELIA AND REED ZARS**	
ACTIVITY	**SKIING, BIKING**	

ABOVE Cordelia at the gate to the homestead.

Zarsian
Adventures

CORDELIA ZARS

I play the last note, snap the book of Beethoven's sonatas shut, and look up at the sky. Yep—it's time to go. I bid my treasured piano goodbye; the one my grandmother bought over 50 years ago and which still lives on my great-grandfather's ranch in northwest Colorado. I grab my mountain bike and point myself in the direction of the old homestead, 12 miles uphill. The homestead has too many temperature swings to house a piano year-round, so I rode down to the ranch for a few hours of practice.

When I make my first turn into a neck-bending headwind, I know I have lingered too long. It's 7pm and the dry heat of the day turns over restlessly. The sky stoops and blankets the landscape in rain. I turn onto the gravel road and pound the pedals uphill.

My great-grandfather set up camp with his cattle here in Colorado back in 1907. The land is a raw kind of beautiful. Sagebrush and antelope, and the parched lips of cracked earth.

My dad, Reed, spent most of his childhood here, between the homestead, the ranch, and nomadic sheep camp. Out here he learned, as his predecessors discovered before him, that you don't get anything without working for it. And although my brothers and I didn't grow up irrigating or running sheep, my dad made sure we didn't get off scot-free.

A FAMILY AFFAIR

"I sought, always, to design trips that were inherently impossible," he said one evening, as I chatted with him on the homestead porch. By this tenet, adventures in my family were not typical. In fact, many of them we now refer to affectionately as "Zars Marches." My older brother describes them as "overcoming adversity with no food."

There was the Thanksgiving we skied from Rabbit Ears Pass to Steamboat—a seven-mile-turned-20-mile bushwacking thrash after we got wildly lost in the waist-deep powder. My dad still won't admit we got lost. (We did.) There were grueling 90-mile days on family tandems through the hellacious Wyoming wind, treks to the bottom of the Grand Canyon, unending summit quests on nearby peaks. At the homestead, thunderstorms chased us on every bike ride, as if my dad had willed them for a little excitement. Caught in heavy rain and hail, the dirt turned to clay and gummed up our tires until we had to ditch the bikes and walk. Soon the clay gummed up our shoes, until they became so heavy we had to ditch them, too. So we'd run, barefoot and sopping wet, back to the cabin. We'd go back the next day to collect the wreckage of abandoned bikes, shoes, and socks.

"I sought, always, to design trips that were inherently impossible," he said one evening, as I chatted with him on the homestead porch.

Being the musical child in my rugged and athletic family didn't spare me from participating in Zars Marches. In fact, the piano became further inspiration for my dad's inventive adventures. His mother played piano, the same piano I practiced on, after long cattle drives and shoveling rattlesnakes off the homestead porch. So in my dad's mind, music and adventure were firmly intertwined.

And as I madly pedal away from the ranch now, thunder echoing around me and Beethoven pounding in my ears, I know they are for me, too. I tighten my grip on the bicycle handlebars and pump my feet on the pedals, as I remember the last piano fiasco from a few years ago. One of my dad's Zars Marches, to the core.

A WINTER MARCH

It began at the homestead. December. Nine degrees outside, snow banked up against the house. My dad and I had skied all over that morning, and I had just curled up by the fire as the sun set.

My dad started whistling. That was the first bad sign. Then walking around the cabin and straightening things. The second. When he tromped up the ladder, rummaged around in the loft, and hollered down at me, "Oh say, Cord…?" I knew the inklings of a Zars March had begun.

I tried ignoring him. No luck. He had dug up my electric keyboard—an archaic, 80-lb behemoth that I'd plug in when we had enough solar power. He yelled down that I must need this in Maine, where I was in college at the time.

"Sure," I said. "But I can come get it in the spring when we can drive in, instead of skiing it 10 miles into town."

His reply was the sound of ropes uncoiling, tarps unfolding, and an unnecessary number of bangs emanating from the floorboards above me. I sighed. As usual, any type of rational negotiation only added fuel to the fire.

Half an hour later we clipped our boots into our skis. My dad wore the hip-strap to the giant orange sled, the keyboard cradled in blankets and tarps within. I was the designated "braker", bungie-corded to the back of the sled to make sure it didn't plow over my dad and kill him as we sailed down our harrowing lane. The keyboard devoured the banks of snow around our skinny ski tracks as we set off into the fading light.

On the uphills I would skitter around my dad and attach my bungee cords to him, to double our power. The western horizon swallowed the sun. The temperature dropped and the air tore at our lungs. Our wax was losing glide. We traded off strapping into the sled, trying to move fast enough to keep our sweat from freezing. Our eyelashes iced over, and we flicked on our headlamps. As my dad skied along gleefully in front of me, I clamped my jaw and swore to myself this would be the last time I ever exercised.

LEGACY
The lightning flashes me back to the present. I am reminded that that winter adventure was not, in fact, the last day I would ever exercise, as I gasped my way up the Continental Divide in flight of a thunderstorm. I sprint the last pitch to the top and fling myself onto the downhill. Rain beats down on my face and arms, and for a moment I'm not sure if it is raining or hailing. I don't know where the lightning is; I can hear it, and feel it, and it's terrifying.

And yet, there's something about it that is nothing short of joy. Something about the thrill of this dance with nature, the unbuckled beauty of the sky, the music of the clouds and the thunder and my heart, pounding. It reminds me of who I am. Who my family has been, for generations.

As usual, any type of rational negotiation only added fuel to the fire.

And as much as we complain about the agony of Zars Marches, my brothers and I also recognize that my dad's adventures are what gave us grit to get through the tough moments in life. It's Zars Marches we credit when our strength makes the mountains seem a little smaller, the daunting miles disappear, and the vertical faces of life emerge with footholds and grips—when we imagine, and dare, to climb.

And as I sail headlong down the hill toward the homestead, my sunglasses streaming with rain, my chest heaving back and forth over the handlebars, all I can do is laugh.

BELOW Cordelia and her father, Reed, ski out of the homestead.

RIGHT Reed slurps a drink at the top of the Continental Divide.

ABOVE Reed strapped to the "giant orange sled" used for transporting many things, including a keyboard.

BELOW Cordelia and Reed at the Zars family homestead in Colorado.

Venga, *Venga*

FITZ CAHALL

Walking among the trees and bird calls of the forest on the edge of her Guadalajara neighborhood, a then 15-year-old Fernanda Rodriguez and her sister stumbled upon a sight they struggled to make sense of. A group of climbers gathered around a large boulder.

"I said to my sister, 'Do you see those guys?'" Fernanda remembers saying as they inched closer to get a better look. "My sister said, 'Yes, they're walking on the rock.' We didn't even know this word 'climbing'."

The climbers noticed the two girls carefully watching through the trees, invited them over, and encouraged them to try. The sisters stared at each other in shock, but Fernanda volunteered. She stepped up to the boulder, timidly asked them how to start, and then followed as they offered advice on where to place her feet and what hold to grab. As she moved up the piece of stone, something flashed inside her.

"I started to feel something inside me, like a flame was lit in my heart," says Fernanda. "Climbing brought me to this amazing feeling of freedom. It allowed me to feel control of my life and be responsible for my own decisions. It showed me a world of possibilities."

A DREAM DEVELOPS

"I used to imagine myself as a great athlete, when I was a child," Fernanda says. "But at that moment, financially… my parents were worried about feeding me and my other four brothers and sisters. Everything else was luxuries, even to go to school."

In the early 2000s, climbing marched toward becoming a truly global sport. Gyms brought climbing to urban areas. Climbers found and developed cliffs and boulders that might have been overlooked or deemed unworthy years before. They hunted for new spots and locales across the globe—and so climbing arrived at the El Diente boulders just north of Guadalajara, ready to be

VENGA, VENGA

LOCATION **EL SALTO, CIENEGA DE GONZÁLEZ, MEXICO**

PEOPLE **FERNANDA RODRIGUEZ**

ACTIVITY **CLIMBING**

LEFT A bird's eye view of Cañón de San Cristóbal in El Salto, Mexico.

discovered by Fernanda. She returned day after day, the act of moving across stone providing an outlet from the cramped apartment she shared with her family. Her sister often joined her and they built friendships with the climbers that frequented the area. After school, they learned to belay, tackling taller and taller walls among the maze of granite boulders and small cliffs, waiting to catch the sunset before scampering home.

At the time, organized sports for girls—particularly in working class areas—were few and far between in Mexico, so climbing provided a physical outlet Fernanda couldn't find anywhere else. When local climbers organized an outdoor bouldering competition around El Diente, a climber mentor nudged Fernanda to participate. When she went to sign up, she discovered the beginning and intermediate categories were full, and that she'd have to compete at the advanced level against some of Mexico's best climbers. She set her nerves aside and focused on each route. Fernanda placed second, winning a pair of new climbing shoes, her first harness, and a month's pass to the climbing gym. More

importantly, a new goal bubbled up inside her head—to become a professional climber.

A FIERCE COMPETITOR
In the years following that first win, Fernanda graduated high school and immediately went to work to support herself. She sold shoes in the plaza. Waitressed. Painted houses. She worked in part to pay for entry and travel to competitions around Mexico, eventually earning a spot on the country's National Team for bouldering. After placing at a series of regional and national competitions, she qualified for the Bouldering World Cup in Vail, CO.

For years, the GoPro Mountain Games have wrapped a rollicking weekend of incredible athleticism across a variety of outdoor sports with a mountain town party. By 2012, competition climbing had begun its long push toward becoming an Olympic sport and the world's best comp climbers came to throw down. After years of relentless training and work, the World Cup was Fernanda's opportunity to make a statement on a global level. Yet her road looked very different from

LEFT Fernanda rests on a stalactite during the first female ascent of Andrada's Project in El Salto, Mexico.

RIGHT Fernanda moving delicately on the limestone wall.

"Climbing brought me to this amazing feeling of freedom... It showed me a world of possibilities."

those of her fellow competitors. The Mexican Climbing Federation had just enough to pay for her plane ticket to Colorado. Fernanda would need to figure out the rest.

Arriving with high expectations, Fernanda realized almost immediately that she was surrounded by climbers whose entire lives were focused on performing at competition. Many of them had been climbing since early childhood, grew up in families that climbed, or trained at internationally renowned training facilities. Sponsorship allowed some to climb full-time and regularly travel without support from USA Climbing. Some had been competing internationally in the World Cup series for years. Fernanda placed 24th in a field that included some of the greatest female competition climbers of all time. Among the podium finishers that day, two would go on to be 2020 Olympians. She sensed an insurmountable gap.

To a competitor like Fernanda, simply making it to this stage provided no solace. The physical preparation and financial effort had consumed her life leading up to Vail. She had perceived this as her chance to make a statement and capture the attention of sponsors. Instead, another truth became clear—being a top competitor would require training full-time and traveling to more international competitions. She couldn't afford either.

"I saw these girls on the podium, super far away from my possibilities, from my own training, and from my economic situation," says Fernanda. "It was kind of a heartbreak."

NEW HORIZONS

Back home in Mexico, questions churned through Fernanda's mind.

Where had rock climbing gotten her? What had all the years of effort amounted to? Was it time to quit?

"For a long time, I was training with a very clear objective—my challenge was winning a competition, getting on a podium with the Mexican flag, and representing my country with pride," she says. "I said, 'Okay, Fernanda. What's next?'"

She let her mind return to those early days of climbing on the outskirts of Guadalajara. She thought of the wind moving through the trees and the magic of watching the sunset from the cliffs before scampering home. It had felt like freedom. She'd pursued sponsorship for so long that she'd forgotten what sparked that fire a decade before.

"I decided to return to the rocks and rock climbing, with the same passion that I experienced that first day," Fernanda remembers. "Climbing for climbing, for fun, for freedom, for myself."

She quickly found a goal—no Mexican woman had climbed the 5.14 grade. Many consider it a grade that delineates elite climbing. In 2012, worldwide just a few dozen women had achieved that mark in their careers. It requires years of experience, training, and athleticism. It was just beyond her current hardest route but the base fitness she developed for the international competition was at an all time high.

IN REACH

Nestled in a rural canyon south of Monterrey, El Salto's limestone crags are one of North America's premier winter climbing destinations. The highly featured walls often require athletic holds between stalactites on wildly overhanging cliffs. Fernanda set her sights on a 5.14 route, dubbed H-Bomb and named for the hold shaped like an "H". Returning to climbing outside after years of relentless training in stuffy fluorescent-lit gyms, felt wonderful. In the canyon, she worked on deciphering the complex sequences of movement and then practicing them until the route felt in reach.

"I remember coming back to that feeling of connection," remembers Fernanda. "Finally I was in a place where there weren't all these rules. On the rock everything is more personal, a connection to nature and a connection with myself."

After a month's toil unlocking the complicated sequence of moves on the weekends and training during the weeks, Fernanda packed her gear and headed to El Salto. With friends, she wandered up the canyon in the evening light, set up camp beneath the wall, and slept beneath the stars. The flutter of birds announced the dawn and Fernanda awoke, excited and ready to give it her all. Spanish-speaking climbers have a saying— "A muerte", or "to the death". It means to give the whole of yourself to a climb.

Tied in and chalked up, Fernanda looked up at the route, tracing the sequences through. She began climbing upward. First, through a series of easier moves, before the wall steepened and Feranda entered a series of gymnastic, improbable moves. Her fingers curled around tiny holds in the limestone, the slow burn of lactic acid developing crept into her forearms. She rested when possible, slowing her breathing to keep her heart rate low and muscles relaxed.

"I was thinking, 'I want to be the first woman.' To be honest that was my purpose, but also feeling the moves, feeling myself, and taking the time to breathe. I was very happy to be on the rock again."

Fernanda flowed through the movement, battling hard through the route's crux section. Easier, but still difficult climbing remained. A misstep or fall here would be heartbreaking after years of training and a month spent linking this 100ft of improbable moves. From below her friends called out, "¡Venga, venga!", encouraging her upward. Fernanda felt belief and determination flow through her, the same simple joy of moving upward

ABOVE Fernanda linking moves on *Dante's Inferno* in El Salto, Mexico.

that she first sensed years earlier as a 15-year-old stumbling into Guadalajara's boulders. Moving steadily and with attention, she made the final moves, reaching the top and realizing her goal. Cheers echoed across El Salto's canyon walls.

"When I got to the top, I was like, 'Ahhh... this is ecstasy!'" Fernanda says about the moment she achieved her goal. "I said to myself, 'Fernanda, this is the... *como se dice el comienzo*?' This is the beginning. The beginning of your life."

Postscript: After H-Bomb, Fernanda realized her goal of becoming a professional athlete. Today, she is a sponsored climber. She inspires and supports the next generation of Mexican women climbers through instruction and coaching. She climbed her second 5.14 in 2018 and believes she is capable of another.

Adapted from reporting by Cordelia Zars

GO WEST

📍 LOCATION	**ROCKY MOUNTAIN NATIONAL PARK**
PEOPLE	**BRENDAN LEONARD**
ACTIVITY	**ROAD TRIPPING**

ABOVE The Mittens in Arizona's Monument Valley are an iconic symbol of the American West.

Go *West*

BRENDAN LEONARD

RIGHT Brendan with his father, Joe, recreating an image shot on the same bench at Forest Canyon Overlook, 24 years previously.

I roll over onto my right side and peek out the saucer-sized hole I have left in my sleeping bag for breathing. I open a slit of one near-sighted, contact lens-less eye. I make out a world one-third black, one-third glowing orange, and one-third deep blue. I'm still mostly asleep and could have slept for another hour or two, but a sunrise most people only ever see on an office wall calendar was slowly opening up behind the thousand-foot-high East and West Mittens, the centerpieces of Monument Valley, AZ.

The Mittens are American icons. And though most folks probably couldn't tell you where they are on a map, if you showed those same people a photo of the Mittens, they would tell you they're in the United States,

somewhere out West, and probably because of the movies directed by John Ford. The reason I'm here, squinting at them out of a hole in my sleeping bag, isn't because I saw them in *Stagecoach*, but because my father loved Westerns and, through them, inspired in me a love of the West.

THE ROAD TRIP

I grew up in the flat Midwest, in a state where 70 per cent of the ground is covered by corn and soybean plants, and the tallest thing on the horizon was a grain elevator. My dad spoke the words "out west" as if they were capitalized, important, making it holier than any other part of the country. The way other fathers speak of the 1967 Green Bay Packers or the good old days.

In 1973, my dad was 22 years old. After taking a road trip in a Chevy Luv pickup through Colorado, New Mexico, Arizona, and California with his legendary high school buddy Cary, Dad ended up in Loveland, CO, where his sister lived. Loveland is not one of those famous mountain towns, but to a young guy who spent his entire life in a small town in Iowa, it might as well have been Aspen.

"I guess when I left Nebraska, that's when I started looking at the western skyline," says Dad. "And once I caught a glimpse, and I couldn't tell you where exactly we were, it just kept getting better and better."

After a few months of living in Loveland and working at a local grocery store, Dad moved into a drafty trailer in Poudre Park. The Wild and Scenic Poudre River roared by 50ft away from his backdoor, and canyon walls shot up hundreds of feet around it. Rocky Mountain National Park was a few minutes away by car. That year, Robert Redford starred in the mountain-man classic movie *Jeremiah Johnson*. John Denver released an album called *Rocky Mountain High*. His generation's art was steeped in Americana.

But Dad didn't stay. To a kid who grew up poor, security was a bigger priority than the scenery of the Rockies. After a year, he moved back to Iowa, got a good job, and married my mom—Miss Congeniality 1969—in Emmetsburg, IA. My brother arrived in 1977 and I followed in 1979. My dad's career of making people laugh from behind the meat counter of a half-dozen grocery stores provided enough security for us to take a few trips to the mythical West.

"I enjoyed some of the best times of my life in the mountains," he says. "I wanted to make sure that if I experienced it, that you would experience it, and see if you enjoyed it."

I have a photo of my dad and me taken in August 1985, on a bench made out of stacked rocks and sawed timber in Rocky Mountain National Park. The bench is somewhere along Trail Ridge Road, allowing park visitors an incredible view of a collection of peaks along the Continental Divide. My brother snapped that photo. I'm six with blond hair, legs dangling in the air beneath me. My dad would be a young 34 in the photo, and you can tell by the smile on his face that he knows he's in a special place.

WHERE THE COWBOYS LIVE
Doc Holliday. The Sundance Kid. Jeremiah Johnson. Wyatt Earp. These are men who headed west to figure it all out in the big hills or the open country. There aren't so many real cowboys left in America, just lots of folks who dress like them. The best most of us can do is buy a pickup truck or chew tobacco. That was the closest I ever got. Maybe the cowboy is gone, but the tradition of going west to reinvent oneself has endured. At some point, I got the idea that there was something in the mountains worth looking for, and I'd better get out west and look for it. I didn't want a nice house. I wanted my life to look like a movie.

Dad offered to take me to check out the campus at the University of Montana. At the time, I thought he was just trying to be helpful. But when we flew in, over the mountains bear-hugging the town of Missoula, his face lit up like a little kid who was about to meet Mickey Mouse on his first visit to Disneyland. I remembered then how much he had always loved the mountains. I inherited this from him. I moved to Montana and Montana changed me.

The things that make me happy—alpine starts, desert sunsets, exposed ridgelines—are not things that my parents can easily explain to people they meet at parties. I'm sure my dad never goes into work on Monday

At some point, I got the idea that there was something in the mountains worth looking for, and I'd better get out west and look for it. I didn't want a nice house. I wanted my life to look like a movie.

morning and says to the guys, "Well, my youngest son finally led that heinous off-width line at Vedauwoo he's been eyeballing since last summer." I drive a 14-year-old car with 180,000 miles and about 50 dents on it. The replacement value of my outdoor gear is larger than my life savings. I own one tie and have never owned a suit. In the hard-working Iowa I come from, this is not what success looks like.

I have enough hindsight to see that my father has been supportive of mostly everything, even if he disagreed with me. "Got a couple of tattoos? Okay." "A couple more? Okay." "Graduate school? Okay." "Oh, now you're a vegetarian. Whatever makes you happy, son. I'll throw a portabello mushroom on the grill."

Now, several times a year I am in my car, tearing down a highway somewhere in the West, music up too loud, and I have a moment. The hair on the back of my neck stands up and I get a lump in my throat and I push it down with a smile. If I'm by myself, I usually start laughing. I take in whatever's flying by my car windows —red desert towers, snow-flecked peaks, endless pine forests—and I say to myself, "This is exactly what my dad would want me to be doing."

RE-ENACTING THE SCENE
Of course, it never took much to convince my parents to come out west for a visit. From my apartment near downtown Denver, Rocky Mountain National Park was less than a two-hour drive away. So we ended up there a lot, hiking on the trails and stopping at the vistas. And eventually, I wondered, "Is that bench still there?"

You couldn't see more than a hundred feet in front of the windshield as my parents and I drove up Trail Ridge Road in Rocky Mountain National Park on a Saturday in September. One of the first snows of the season was dropping a cloud of flakes everywhere higher than 10,000ft. We kept driving into the snow, higher toward the crest of the road at 12,183ft in my mom's white Toyota sedan with Iowa license plates. We weren't a bunch of lost Midwesterners who didn't know any better than to drive upward into a Rocky Mountain snowstorm. We were just looking for a certain bench.

The snow didn't let up as we strolled from the car down the path to Forest Canyon Overlook, where I had narrowed it down to one of two benches. Dad pulled up the photo—taken in 1985, all of us sitting with the mountains behind—on his BlackBerry so we could make sure. We argued for a couple of minutes about which one we had sat on 24 years ago, then

settled on the first bench on the trail, not too far for a 6-year-old to walk back then.

Mom offered to take the photo this time since my brother was a couple of thousand miles away, raising their first grandchild and preparing for the arrival of another. No film or flash cubes this time. You can't see anything but a giant wall of white behind us in the new shot. Fat snowflakes are falling all over us, making the whole thing look hazy. I look older than I think I should, and Dad would probably say the same thing about himself. I wonder if he ever thought he'd be back here with me, or if he thought I'd be a doctor instead of a dirtbag by now.

I'm not sure what dreams Dad had for his kids in 1985, but I guess most parents just want their children to be happy. I don't get back to visit as often as I should. That's partly his fault and partly Jeremiah Johnson's, but mostly it's due to whatever it is in some of us that has to go out there and take a good long look so we can find out what's inside. Because my dad put the West up on a pedestal, I'm here living what I think is a dream. And I'm the happiest guy I know.

Three
Wheelin'

FITZ CAHALL

LEFT Welcome to Iowa, home of RAGBRAI, the oldest and longest multi-stage bike event in the world.

There was no pool or ocean, but Caleb Smith decided, tactically speaking, that Speedo briefs were the best clothing option for this adventure. Heat would be an issue. It was early Sunday morning in small-town Iowa. A grid of cornfields and rolling hills stretched out in front of him. A few cyclists rolled past, craning their necks in puzzlement.

"I'm standing in a parking lot with these skin-tight briefs and I'm just like, 'What am I doing right now?'" remembers Caleb. "I was just so embarrassed for what was about to happen to me. Down the highway, the sun was coming up and it was green on both sides. I sat there for so long and then finally I was like, 'I got to do this.' I put my skates on and started to mosey down the road. It was the feeling of jumping into water. The next thing you know, I was just doing it."

The 'it' was RAGBRAI, an acronym for the Register's Annual Great Bicycle Ride Across Iowa. Founded by a local newspaper in 1973, this annual event is the world's oldest, largest, and longest multi-day bicycle touring event. It cannot be stated emphatically enough—this is not a race. It is an experience. Caleb was about to make the most out of that experience. It is very unlikely that anyone had ever even thought to in-line skate the entire route, and even more unlikely that anyone had followed through with the idea.

In the mid-1990s, in-line roller skating swept the nation, with children and adults adopting it for both play and fitness. Aggressive in-line skating took a skateboarding mentality and turned the sport up to 11. Cityscapes became playgrounds where skaters leapt over flights of stairs and slid down handrails. In-line skating helped drive viewership to the burgeoning X-Games before being unceremoniously dropped from the lineup. As a young kid, Caleb got swept up in the sport and the community that surrounded it in Iowa. As he grew up and his friends sought less dangerous pastimes, as

THREE WHEELIN'

📍 LOCATION	**IOWA**	
PEOPLE	**CALEB SMITH**	
ACTIVITY	**IN-LINE SKATING**	

ABOVE Twenty thousand cyclists complete RAGBRAI each year—and one in-line skater.

Having control over your own mind and your own thoughts will take you so much farther than all the best equipment, all the best training.

they followed careers and started families, Caleb kept skating. So when his girlfriend signed up for RAGBRAI, his instinct was not to bike, but skate.

DIPPING THE WHEELS
July in Iowa is hot, muggy, and decidedly unpleasant —but that does nothing to dampen the cyclists' spirits as they dip their front tire in the Missouri River, then begin pedaling east. Organizers switch up the route every year, bringing the party to eight small towns, who turn out to celebrate and feed the riders. City parks become campgrounds. Farmers' barns host parties stretching deep into the night. Civic groups cook up tens of thousands of pancakes. Food trucks sprout up in schoolyards. On average, the week-long route covers 470 miles. Typically, around 20,000 cyclists complete the voyage each year, but 60,000 cyclists showed up for one of the legs to celebrate the ride's 50th anniversary in 2023. At the end of the week, successful riders touch their wheels into the Mississippi River to mark the journey's end.

In 2017, Caleb dipped his wheels, then began powering out long graceful strides as the temperature on the blacktop crept up. Hoots, hollers, and quizzical looks ensued as bikers passed.

He planned... sort of. In fairness, Caleb was in uncharted territory. In the weeks leading up to RAGBRAI, Caleb skated 6–8 miles each day. Blissfully ignorant and happy with his progress, he turned his attention to tactics. He knew it would be very hot. He would start earlier than most. To beat the heat he brought two pieces of clothing—a pair of basketball shorts and a Speedo. He found a team of young artists and musicians (dubbed "Dude Storm") who he could camp and carpool with from the start to the finish. He had a vision.

Slightly self-conscious about his uniform decision, Caleb learned the traditions of RAGBRAI. As people pass other riders, it's customary to slow down and share a conversation before heading on. He skated past the "Mile of Silence", where a hush falls over riders as they remember the 30 riders and volunteers that have lost their lives participating in this event. Gentle chiding from fellow travelers converted Caleb into a helmet wearer, something that was stylistically shunned in the aggressive in-line skating crowd, which was fortunate because he crashed that first afternoon, leaving his body covered in road rash.

LEFT The RAGBRAI biking community convinced Caleb to wear a helmet.

FIGHTING FOR EVERY INCH
Caleb skated 62 miles that first day—more than twice as far as he'd ever skated before—and he needed to do that for six more days. What was moderately challenging on a bicycle was herculean on in-line skates. Body protesting from the crash and previous miles, he powered through 72 miles the next day as he began to understand the tiny nuances of every muscle in his body and how to relax them. Cramps racked his body and he slowly made adjustments in his stride and posture. The community pulled him forward. In front of farmhouses, smiling children ran peanut butter and jelly sandwich aid stations. Coolers filled with cold beer and drinks magically appeared atop hills. At a giant makeshift swimming pool created by the local fire department, Caleb arrived to cheers. Word had spread about the Speedo-clad skater. On day three, modesty getting the better of him, Caleb decided to don the basketball shorts—but then a group of mom riders encouraged him to go back to the Speedo.

By day four, everyone is feeling the back-to-back days of movement, but Caleb's body was in catharsis and the emotional highs he had felt fell away to valleys. A bicycle overcomes hills via mechanical advantage, but skating meant fighting for every inch. Rain poured down. He huddled with other riders under a makeshift tent as the worst of the storm passed, but he knew that he had to give up on the day. A wave of dejection washed over him, as if he'd failed. The following morning back spasms struck and, knowing that he wouldn't complete his envisioned in-line skating ultramarathon if he didn't stop now, he took a rest day in hopes of salvaging the final two. This was a perfect experience, a physical test of limits, among an incredible group of people in a special landscape.

NOT SO FLAT
"I feel like everyone's surprised at how much I love Iowa," says Caleb. "You have to experience it firsthand because most people, they end up just passing through. They drive through it on the interstate, but it's like this multifaceted place with so much beauty that's just hidden around every corner."

The snootiest outdoors people might refer to the Hawkeye State as fly-over country, best seen out of the window of a plane. Cornfields as far as the eye don't lend themselves to adventure—and yet, here was Caleb, redefining how to travel a landscape and expanding his own horizon of what was physically possible.

On day six, the hills appeared like waves. Caleb crested up over the undulating fields alongside his fellow travelers. He'd refined his technique, dialing in his uphill cadence and then resting on the descents to recoup energy. The last day offered 3,200ft of climbing over 45 miles. Before this week, in his decade-plus of skating, he'd never tried anything at this type of scale. The feeling that he'd somehow failed by not completing all seven days faded and a window into what he was capable of appeared. Cresting the final hill of the day, Caleb paused, surrounded by people from around the world who'd come here for RAGBRAI. Emotion swelled inside him. This experience extended much deeper than any definition of the fun that Caleb had previously had. A week of hanging out with friends and community evolved into something life-changing.

Caleb pointed the skates down the last long hill into the city of Lansing and the banks of the Mississippi. The hill seemed to stretch forever; one last reward for the struggle. Along Main Street, people cheered from porches and two-story store fronts. Kids offered popsicles and adults offered congratulations. Sadness and relief simultaneously swept through Caleb, followed by something that felt like victory, though softened by humility. Transcendence by in-line. He remembered the start, seven days earlier. Waves of nervousness rolled over him as he looked down the road.

"I think I knew I was getting into something much bigger than a ride across Iowa. That feeling, that magic of RAGBRAI, swept over me the whole course of the week," he recalls. "RAGBRAI taught me about myself, that willpower and mindset are more important than physical strength. Having control over your own mind and your own thoughts will take you so much farther than all the best equipment, all the best training."

Postscript: After his first RAGBRAI, Caleb continued his love affair with long-distance skating and pioneered the new discipline of Ultra Skating. He's gone on to skate more than 200 miles in a day, completed long-distance routes between midwest cities, and envisioned routes in iconic landscapes like Death Valley. He's completed RAGBRAI every year since 2017 with the company of other skaters. As a sponsored athlete, he helps new skaters find their stride.

Adapted from reporting by Cordelia Zars and Ashlee Langholz

Adventures *with Bozarth*

LAUREN DELAUNAY MILLER

My three-year, love-hate relationship with my Ford Explorer had just ended. Something about the axles being ready to fall off at any minute. After weeks of a car-less existence, bumming rides up and down the canyons outside Colorado's Estes Park had gotten old. I scanned Craigslist for a car that was big enough to also call home. I expanded my search radius every day that I didn't find one in my budget. Then, I saw it: a 1997 Chevy Astro Van. Low miles, just one owner, and a price I could afford. I hitched one last ride down the canyon to Boulder, hopped on a bus to Denver, walked to the Greyhound station, and headed west toward Grand Junction. I had no return ticket.

The van's owner, a grandmother of 12, kept the kind of meticulous records that mechanics dream about. She handed me the keys and a logbook of van activity, including every time she filled the gas tank for the past 20 years. Soon, I was back on I-70 heading home, as free as I had ever been.

LEFT That freedom feeling in a car big enough to call home.

I was entering that van as a directionless caterpillar, but one day, I'd emerge as the brave independent person I wanted to be.

ADVENTURES WITH BOZARTH

📍 LOCATIONS	**COLORADO; MOAB, UT; YOSEMITE VALLEY, CA; AND BISHOP, CA**
PEOPLE	**LAUREN DELAUNAY MILLER**
ACTIVITY	**CLIMBING, ROAD TRIPPING**

ABOVE A climber on the Half Dome in the Yosemite National Park.

The van even had its own name, declared on a sticker right under the rear windshield: Bozarth #1. With my new home on wheels, I knew I'd soon enjoy endless days of climbing and perfect nights curled up in my very own cocoon.

A FIT-OUT, OF SORTS

Back in Estes, I got to work on some renovations. Bozarth had that distinct "vintage" smell, and the only way I could figure to get rid of it once and for all was to rip everything out. The bench seats went to the dump, along with the floor-to-ceiling carpet. All that remained was a metal box. Imagining that I would travel primarily in warm places, I skimped on bulky insulation in favor of headspace. Then, I started on the bed, building the frame to my exact length. To save money, I shoved a socket wrench in my glovebox instead of installing a slick swivel for the passenger seat. Whenever I wanted the chair to face a different direction, I could simply unscrew the bolts, turn the chair around, and bolt it back down. I was entering that van as a directionless caterpillar, but one day, I'd emerge as the brave, independent person I wanted to be.

Or so I thought. I migrated to Moab, UT, for the winter, giddy about the climbing I'd do. I did not anticipate how wildly the desert winter temperatures would swing. So while I ran trails in Canyonlands and climbed splitter cracks in Indian Creek under the still-warm desert sun, I also spent my nights cursing the fact that I'd rushed through the "insulation" stage of my van renovation. I had to turn on my little propane heater just to get myself out from under my two down sleeping bags.

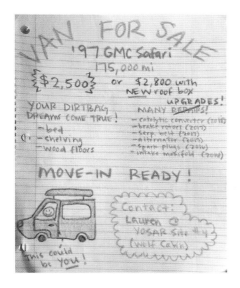

RIDING SHOTGUN

Halfway through the winter, I found myself hopelessly in love. I stationed Bozarth in the parking lot outside the gear shop where my new boyfriend worked. But even all the snug nights on a bed built for one couldn't save that relationship. When it went up in smoke weeks later, I stared at the miniature Christmas stockings I had hung up for us and filled the 9-sq-ft of floor space with crumpled tissues. Bozarth might have been my #1, but I couldn't help but look for someone to ride shotgun.

Spring arrived, and I felt my heartache thaw with the longer days. Free to roam, I pointed my wheels toward California. Bozarth soared on familiar turns through the Sierra Nevada. We passed granite slabs, lakes like glass, trees too big to wrap your arms around, and finally swooped down into Yosemite Valley. I showed up feeling strong, but when I signed myself up for a huge climbing mission with my friend Josie, we got instantly stifled by the heat. We retreated to the Valley floor to soothe our dehydrated bodies in the river, where she introduced me to her friend, Bud.

Before long, I got swept away again, and began spending most of my time in Bud's employee housing. It wasn't exactly a place I could call my own, though, and I made a point to never bring my things inside. I visited Bozarth each morning and gathered my climbing gear for the day. Bud and I committed to a house for the winter, but I still couldn't bear to give up Bozarth or the freedom he allowed me. If this relationship vanished, too, I knew Bozarth would catch me. So even though Bozarth spent most of the winter parked in the driveway, I didn't consider letting him go.

The following spring, I started to get sick of a few of Bozarth's "unique" traits. The alternator went on the fritz again, even though I had replaced it twice that winter. The oil leaked, and the lack of air conditioning became a real issue in the desert heat. Bud and I planned a trip to bask in the warm sandstone of Red Rock Canyon, and I feared this might be one of the last trips Bozarth and I would take together. On our third day, I felt the all-too-familiar stomach jolt when the check engine light turned on. I soon found myself in downtown Las Vegas confronting an expensive mechanic's bill. With no other choice, I forked over the money so we could get back home.

On our way back to Yosemite, as Mount Wilson faded in the rearview mirror, we approached a huge neon sign. Its words glowed unmistakably: "Bozarth #1". As I drove past countless cars in the paved lots of Ed

Bozarth Chevrolet, I realized there were thousands of Bozarths, each with their own identical sticker claiming to be #1. I felt deceived. My Bozarth wasn't really #1.

But as the miles stretched on toward California, I couldn't help but laugh. My van would always be #1 to me.

THE ROAD AHEAD

That summer, as Bud and I settled into a new home together, I knew the time had come. I ripped a piece of paper from my notebook, and with a box of crayons, drafted Bozarth's "For Sale" flyer. I taped it to the board in Camp 4, a popular trading post for Yosemite climbers. Soon I had a buyer—a couple planning a winter road trip across the West, and this was their dream rig.

In the years since, Bud and I got married. We renovated a vintage tow-behind camper—a much more spacious option for the two of us and our 70-lb dog. I don't miss the constant dread that Bozarth might break down at any second. Still, every time I see an Astro Van flying down Tioga Pass or puttering along dirt tracks in the desert, I think about that first day I took Bozarth home. I wave to each Astro pilot I pass, imagining that they're using their wheels to chase the best that each season has to offer.

I felt scared that giving up Bozarth meant giving up my freedom. But moving forward in my relationship meant stepping in with both feet and trading my escape hatch for a hatchback. And yet, every few months, I'll feel that call to hit the road on my own. Even if I have to curl up in the back of my Prius to do it.

Chapter Two
Going Big, Feeling Small

Just Make *It Happen*

JEN ALTSCHUL

At 19, I interviewed to be a ski patroller with Oregon's Mount Hood Meadows. "I've been skiing for eight years," I told the director. "I can get down just about anything, some things with more grace than others." The rest of the interview must have gone well. She caught my arm as I walked out of the job fair—I had the position if I wanted it.

I didn't exactly lie about my skiing ability, but I definitely didn't tell the whole truth. I'd been skiing for eight years, but on a good year I'd put in maybe 10 days. I could get down just about anything standing up, but only if I slipped slowly enough. I wasn't being intentionally deceptive. I just hadn't seen enough to know how much of a gaper I was.

LEARNING THE ROPES

During pre-season orientation, our coordinator gave us the rundown of our training deadlines. By the end of the first week, we had to load and unload a chairlift with a 60-lb toboggan. By the end of the second week, we had to ski an empty toboggan to anywhere in the resort, and a toboggan with the patient in it down any of the groomed runs. By the end of the month, we

should have been able to assist an injured guest anywhere on the mountain, probe a buried transceiver in under three minutes, and pass a ski test.

I was nervous. I still hadn't wrapped my head around loading a chairlift with a backpack, much less an awkward, person-length Plexiglass sled. I simply couldn't comprehend driving a toboggan down a double black diamond even without a person in it—mainly because I had never actually looked down a double black diamond before. The signs at the gate mentioned cliffs, waterfalls, and experts only. So I had always given the boundaries a little extra berth; like I thought that if I got too close to the orange rope line, I might inadvertently wind up on top of a cliff. Still, I figured that they had hired me and they would teach me what I needed to know. If they thought those deadlines were reasonable, they knew better than I did. So I moved into my first-ever apartment, purchased my first-ever pair of skis, and waited for the snow to hit.

IN THE DEEP END

The snow started and we got hammered. So did my naive confidence.

JUST MAKE IT HAPPEN

📍 LOCATION	**MOUNT HOOD MEADOWS, OR**
PEOPLE	**JEN ALTSCHUL**
ACTIVITY	**SKIING, PATROLLING**

ABOVE Who wouldn't want to work in mountains covered in fresh snow?

"Just Make It Happen" was printed on the back of the patrol sweatshirts because there was no "almost" in putting a rope line up before 8.55am or getting a patient safely down the hill. On my first week, Randy—one of the veteran patrollers—took me out to get acquainted with the terrain. I stood at the top of a moderately steep, relatively short black diamond and watched him link a series of four textbook turns through the early season snow. He turned to wait for me at the bottom. I took a deep breath, pushed myself off the lip, and proceeded to trip over my tips, tomahawk down a quarter of the run, and lose both of my skis. It took me five minutes to retrieve them and click back in. I did this twice more before I finally made it to the bottom, covered in snow and mortified.

Randy shook his head, looking thoroughly unimpressed. I realized that these people, many of whom had been patrolling for half as long as I had been alive, weren't going to stand around patiently coaching me into the patroller they knew I could be. They expected me to prove myself. And I had just failed the first of many tests.

Randy's reaction was subtle compared to the others. A training coordinator threatened to put me in ski lessons. A snow-safety director asked me if I knew I had to pass a ski test. My supervisor told me to "Harden the fuck up!" as he tacked something else onto my project list.

POWER OF PERSISTENCE
I spent the next few months scared. I woke up scared when my alarm would go off at 4.45am. Drove to work scared that my '88 Volvo wagon would get stuck or spin off the road, again. I spent my days scared of falling, scared of missing a turn and ending up on the wrong run, and mostly scared of disappointing my coworkers. By the time I got home in the evening, damp and too exhausted to do anything but eat and sleep, I was already scared for the next morning.

I have no idea why I didn't quit. I thought about it a few times a day. My fellow rookies encouraged me not to give up. And there were other small acts of kindness. The incredible patience of my director. Empathy from a few of the female patrollers. Or the time a second year patroller spent 20 minutes helping me click back into my snow-caked bindings that had fallen off as I slogged through heavy snow because the DIN we set was so low. I stayed, in part, simply because I didn't know what I would do if I left. And, in part, because I had never failed so epically at anything in my life.

I resolved to avoid my coworkers by spending as much time outside as possible. I started making my own project lists, mental notes of signs to fix, rope lines to de-ice, tower pads to dig out of the snow, and doing them all before anyone could tell me to. When someone did ask me to do something, I would just nod and click back into my skis.

Something happened in the process. It wasn't a distinct turning point. More like, one morning riding up the chairlift to our daily debrief, I caught myself mesmerized by the silhouette of the haul rope against the white snow and the orange and red clouds of the sunrise. I was vaguely startled when I realized that for those eight minutes I hadn't thought about the rest of the day, or been terrified of what was to come. I felt lucky.

By the time spring finally fought its way out from under the snowy wrath of La Niña, I stayed on top of my skis more often. I got more confident driving toboggans. I ran through a flawless medical scenario and got my clearance to tend to injured patients. The head of the snow safety kicked me out of the patrol headquarters before opening one morning to go collect my powder paycheck. The yelling matches got quieter. The following season, my training coordinator drove me to Napa Auto Parts to get a new battery for my car, and then insisted on taking me grocery shopping and to the yarn store when it turned out that the battery wasn't the issue. My third season, I dragged more injured guests off of the hill than any other patroller. I stood at the top of a steep bowl in the middle of a whiteout with Randy; then followed him down some of the best powder turns of my life and found him waiting at the bottom, grinning like a little boy. My fourth season, I stopped by my supervisor's house to bake a batch of cookies.

After four winters of ski patrolling, I moved to Seattle to finish my bachelor's degree and could only patrol on my breaks from school. I miss that family every day. While I don't have any desire to relive that first season, I'm honestly grateful for what I went through: yard sales, yelling matches, and all. Not only did it turn me into a capable patroller, it also forced me into a thick skin. And taught me that whatever mashed potatoes I find myself tripping through, I can find a way to make it happen.

"Just Make It Happen" was printed on the back of the patrol sweatshirts because there was no "almost" in putting a rope line up before 8.55am or getting a patient safely down the hill.

Ditch *Logic*

FITZ CAHALL

"See the white picket fence? Stop there," says Gregg Bleakney.

We pull up in front of a large-for-Seattle modern home in a sought-after neighborhood. We are parked in front of his old life.

"Why do you need four bathrooms?" Gregg muses, looking out the car window. "I had the ultimate TV surround-sound system. This black, Italian leather couch. I think that was five grand. I had the new sports car. A garage full of outdoor toys I'd never really used because I didn't know how to use them because I never went outside. Life as a software salesman is about selling things to people, earning your commission—and then your boss tries to encourage you to spend that commission, so you have to go out and make more. It's about earning and buying. At least in my world that's what it was about."

QUARTER-LIFE CRISIS

It was 2005. At 30 years old, Gregg was a software sales exec with a serious girlfriend and a clear road map for life laid out in front of him.

"For some reason, it just didn't feel right," he remembers. "I couldn't figure out why. The money was great. People were great. I was excited about going to work, but something just felt wrong."

At night he couldn't sleep. He'd stay up late, shuffling around the house listening to music before falling asleep watching TV on the big screen. Gregg couldn't remember exactly when the idea snuck into his head. Yet, over the course of three years, it began to consume his thoughts. He told no one. He saved money and traced details, putting an idea into action in total secrecy to avoid being talked out of it or hurting the people he cared about.

DITCH LOGIC

📍	LOCATIONS	**ALASKA TO ARGENTINA**
	PEOPLE	**GREGG BLEAKNEY**
	ACTIVITY	**BICYCLING**

ABOVE Gregg's first photo of the trip with the Salmon Glacier in Alaska behind him.

"When I did stomach the strength to tell my parents, I drove over to their house," Gregg recalls with the look of someone reliving an awkward memory. "I told them, 'I got to talk to you about something.' My mom stood up, clapped her hands and said, 'Oh my gosh, you're getting married.' I said, 'Not exactly mom… and actually I'm quitting my job, selling everything I own, and riding my bike from Alaska to Argentina.'"

THE GREAT NORTH

Prudhoe Bay, AK, to the very tip of South America is a 19,000 mile journey—one of the planet's longest. The "conventional" route follows the Pan American Highway, a network of roads first conceived of in the 1920s for automobiles, and slowly realized with the growth of globalization and road building. Today, a few very committed cyclists complete the journey using a parallel network of backroads and two-lane highways better suited to cycling. Because it crosses so many latitudes, the route covers a staggering array of ecosystems, from Arctic tundra and high deserts, to jungles and windswept fjords. The devoted must figure out how to bypass the Darién Gap, a wild stretch of marshland and mountainous rainforest separating Panama and Colombia, and a lawless corridor where desperate migrants now cross on foot as they head for the US border. This 66 miles is the only section that remains roadless.

ABOVE Crossing the Salar de Uyuni salt flats in Bolivia.

Gregg and his friend Brooks Allen set an ambitious agenda: pedal six solid days a week for a year. There wouldn't be a lot of time to wander off course; eventually both of them would need to get back to Seattle and the real world of significant others and jobs. Their clearly defined sabbatical had a beginning and an end.

In the summer of 2005, the two friends started pedaling south. The first few hundred miles followed the large gravel highway connecting the Arctic Ocean to Fairbanks, AK. The tires relentlessly churned up mud from the roadway. At night, covered in grime, they'd crawl into sleeping bags and a tent alongside the road or beneath bridges. Occasionally, they'd settle for a ditch, simply to escape the wind.

Gregg eased into a new pace. On a particularly rainy Alaskan day, Gregg and Brooks set out to engineer a proper bike fender so that the person following wouldn't get blasted by mud. Gregg found an old plastic milk jug in a ditch and started carving it into a workable mud guard when it hit him.

"Before that, I felt like I was just kind of biking along and I wasn't really on the journey and this wasn't really me," Gregg says. "I was just still sitting in my cubicle or in a suit pitching some client. The trip—all of a sudden —was real."

On the gerry-rigged bike fender, Gregg etched a road and a mountain range, and wrote "Alaska to Argentina". Something in his mind shifted.

SOUTHBOUND

Greg and Brooks cycled southeast out of Alaska, crossing in and out of Canada, then pedaled down the Douglas-fir-lined backroads of the West Coast's small towns. Past the redwoods of northern California, they headed to San Francisco before continuing along the Pacific Coast Highway into Big Sur's fog-draped hills that tailed into the ocean. After San Diego, they crossed the southern border toward the vehicular chaos of Mexico City. Ahead of schedule, a slowed-down sense of euphoria and confidence set in.

"We were two gringos conquering Mexico on our bikes and nothing could stop us," Gregg says. "We'd been warned that the route ahead was dangerous and that there had been problems, but we didn't care."

The southern state of Chiapas had been haunted by political and narco violence, and poverty, for decades. Here, the arbitrariness of a line on a map met with the

world's harsh realities. On a remote backroad, Gregg and Brooks stumbled into an ambush.

"These guys came out of the woods with masks and machetes, and were on us before we could get away," Gregg remembers. "We didn't know what to do, but this guy had a machete at my neck and he was telling me to give him everything I had. I thought, 'Perhaps I could be killed here."

Adrenaline surging, unsure if Brooks was okay, Gregg's mind churned, but then suddenly went calm. As long as they were not hurt, the rest would not matter. The gear the men stole could be replaced. Once free, they could get to safety. Doing his best to remain calm and de-escalate the situation, Gregg felt the danger slide over them like a wave and pass.

"I had this epiphany—everything is going to be fine. You just need to keep going, but I could no longer be naive about the situations around me," says Gregg. "It burst my bubble."

Traumatized but unhurt, Gregg and Brooks regrouped. This wasn't a sabbatical. It was life. In the real world. With real consequences. Gregg's family begged him to come home. Brooks decided it was time to head back.

"He had something to go back to. He had something that was really important to him at that point," Gregg reflects. "The dreams that we had of doing this trip together and finishing together didn't exist anymore."

THIS PAGE Descending the east slope of 15,640ft. Paso de Portachuelo in Peru's Cordillera Blanca, Huascaran National Park.

ALONE AND AFRAID

Gregg kept pedaling, but saddled with the trauma of his robbery, he struggled with constant fear. In the Central American agrarian economies, everyone carried machetes. He passed through Guatemala and then into Honduras, where it wasn't uncommon to see armed groups in the backs of trucks. Gregg's pace slowed. He joined other bicyclists to help with the rising anxiety. He gave up the schedule and the hopes of completing the journey in a year.

A fellow cyclist he met loaned him a camera, and Gregg started taking pictures of people as a coping mechanism, but the camera almost became a wall between him and the people he was meeting and interacting with. Another traveler he met on the road, sensing Gregg was hiding behind the camera, offered a bit of advice.

"Ninety-nine per cent of the people you meet on the road are good people. Go talk to them. They're curious. They're staring at you because you are a gringo on a bicycle. They're not staring at you because they want to rob you," Gregg remembers his friend saying. "I took his advice and it was amazing. I was invited to people's

ABOVE Taking a pause after crossing into Argentinian Patagonia.

homes. Invited to weddings. I made friends. I learned Spanish."

By the time he ferried around the Darién Gap, it had been a year of pedaling. Gregg's approach and perspective had changed. He teamed up with other cyclists he met along the way, to follow side roads. One year turned into two. His relationship dissolved. He stopped worrying whether he would be able to get a job when he returned to Seattle.

NO GOING BACK

"I realized I couldn't go back to my old life," says Gregg. "It wouldn't work for me anymore. I had this clarity of mind where I was like 'You're not going back. You're moving forward. You're taking a new direction, I put the stamp on that by selling my house. It was the last thing I had connecting me."

He closed the deal via satellite phone in a tiny Patagonian outpost. A few hundred miles remained and Gregg had no idea what came next. He kept pedaling further south into the fabled Patagonian peaks that pushed up from the pampas like teeth on a saw blade. Travelers come to the tiny village of El Chaltén from around the world to witness the dawn ignite these granite towers in blinding orange light. These peaks were Yvon Chouinard's inspiration when he founded the clothing company Patagonia.

For three days, dawn broke clear, illuminating the massif. To avoid the infamous Patagonia winds, Gregg slept in a ditch alongside the old gravel road leading to El Chaltén.

On that third morning, as he organized his gear for the day's journey, the milk-carton mud-flap with the hand-drawn mountain detached. The wind plucked it up. Gregg ran down the road after it, emotion unexpectedly rising. It disappeared down the track.

"It was gone, but when I looked up I realized that the scene in front of me was almost exactly the same as what I'd drawn on that mudguard more than a year ago," Gregg remembers. "This was where I was supposed to be. For me at that moment, it didn't even matter if I finished the trip. I went back to the ditch, crawled into my sleeping bag, and just watched the sunrise. This is my new life. I found it."

Postscript: A few weeks later, Gregg reached South America's southern tip. In the ensuing years, Gregg turned his new-found passion for photography into a career, before eventually settling down in Bogotá, Colombia, where he works in film and marketing.

THE UNDERDONKEY

LOCATION   **COLORADO**

PEOPLE   **MARVIN SANDOVAL**

ACTIVITY   **BURRO RACING**

ABOVE Burro racing links long-distance running with Colorado's Gold Rush history.

The Under*Donkey*

FITZ CAHALL

"When she's out there running, she's like a fire-breathing dragon," says Marvin Sandoval.

"She's a little bit wild. I've actually been kicked in every race I've done with her."

The "dragon" in question goes by the name Buttercup. She has long, fuzzy ears, a mane shaped like a mohawk, and when not "breathing fire" enjoys head scratches and pats. Diminutive for the competitive circuit, Buttercup stands no taller than a Great Dane, but has quickly become the most dominant athlete in her discipline.

Welcome to the fringe sport of Burro Racing.

A SPORT EMERGES

Originating in the Colorado mountains, burro races are part endurance event, part homage to the pioneering spirit of the men and women who came West to tap into the mining booms of the 1800s. Until 2020, rules required a racing burro to carry a regulation pack saddle, pickaxe, shovel, and gold pan the length of the course. The racing element harkens back to the dash to town a miner would make after finding gold or silver to stake their claim. While mining no longer dominates the landscape or economy, Colorado has experienced another boom. Call it the endorphin rush.

As more people showed up for long-distance mountain biking, trail runs, and backcountry skiing, outdoor sports offered faltering mining towns like Leadville and Buena Vista, CO, a second chance at a working economy. Burro races bridged the gap between new and old.

Races range from five to 30 miles. Rules are simple. Utilizing a 10–15 ft lead rope, runners run behind, in front of, or alongside their burro. There is absolutely no riding of burros. Racers can push, pull, and, in a truly "break glass in case of emergency" situation, carry their burro. If runner and burro get separated, which happens

when a burro decides to sprint all-out downhill, the pair must return to the point where the runner dropped the lead rope. Most racers typically rent or borrow a burro.

"You better pack a lunch when you're dealing with donkeys because you're on what we call 'Donkey Time,'" says Brad Wann of the pun-friendly Western Pack Burro Ass-ociation. "It ain't your plan. It's not even your race. You're the GPS and it's your job to navigate them through this course."

The novelty of partnering with *Equus asinus* brought the hardcore runners to Colorado. The racers start in quintessential small towns, red brick or colorfully painted buildings of a bygone era, before heading onto dirt roads and trails that slowly climb into the high country. Here aspen leaves flutter in afternoon winds. As trails climb upward, the massive aspen groves give way to meadows filled with summer wildflowers. Afternoon thunderstorms scrape the high alpine talus fields with almost daily clockwork precision. Slowly but surely, the races grew from a history lesson and party trick into an outright competitive circuit, complete with elite athletes and devotees.

Enter Marvin and Buttercup.

THE STAGE IS SET
Marvin found endurance racing in a middle age doldrum. He'd grown up around the world-famous Leadville Trail 100 ultramarathon and mountain biking races, which remain bucket list items for endurance athletes elite and recreational alike, but they felt like an activity for the masochistic, not a journey he'd knowingly sign up for.

"I wouldn't say I was in a bad place in life, but just in a down place," Marvin remembers. "I was driving through town. It just happened that the Leadville Trail 100 bike race starts and finishes in downtown."

Marvin watched a friend come across the finish line. It lit a fire. The next year he completed the 100 mile mountain bike race. Then he moved onto the Lead Challenge—a series of races including a 50- and then 100-mile mountain bike ride, a trail marathon, and 10k run capped by a 100-mile run, all occurring over the course of two months in the high alpine of the Rockies. He won the race series outright in 2015. Then a friend talked him into signing up for a 7-mile burro race with an ass named Stormtrooper. They crossed the finish line in ninth place, but Marvin was hooked.

Then a friend talked [Marvin] into signing up for a seven-mile burro race with an ass named Stormtrooper.

"It's very challenging, because you're at the mercy of this wild animal," says Marvin. "It's not like you can tell the donkey to run or to run alongside of you. Whatever they're interested in at that point in time, they're going to do it."

Marvin discovered another wrinkle to the sport. A non-native species originally from Africa, burros escaped captivity and now populate the American West in wild herds. They've thrived—so much so that they've left land managers scrambling to manage their impact on the ecosystems and other native species. A debate over euthanasia erupted in 2016 before the Bureau of Land Management backed down on the program to kill thousands of wild horses and donkeys, and instead began capturing and auctioning off wild burros to private individuals.

Interest piqued, Marvin and his wife Lisa attended an auction in Arizona. They came home with two burros, Ricky Bobby and Napoleon Dynamite, who they trained

to walk, and then run, on a lead. It wasn't a giant leap when their daughter Jules asked to run a donkey. Worried that a full-size burro would be too much, Marvin went looking for a miniature donkey in New Mexico for his daughter to train.

"I go into the corral," remembers Marvin. "Buttercup comes up to me and I was like, 'This is the one.' I just never pictured running her in a race because she was so small, cute, and cuddly. I didn't think she would ever be good at it."

BUTTERCUP STEPS UP
Desperation led Marvin to line up with Buttercup for the 10-mile Donkey Dash in Creede, CO, in 2019. Snickers, his regular running partner, developed a limp two days prior. Concerned their other two donkeys were pregnant, Marvin asked Jules if he could run with Buttercup. At the starting line, a fellow competitor eyed them up.

"He looked at Buttercup," recalls Marvin "He looked at me, and says, 'I don't think you should be toward the front because you might get run over.' I was like, 'We'll be good.'"

Buttercup had never raced. They finished third.

"I was like, 'I'm sorry Jules, but Buttercup is my donkey now,'" Marvin jokes.

A TASTE OF VICTORY

That summer, the world's best burro racers and thousands of spectators poured into the small town of Fairplay, CO, for the 71st Annual World Championship Pack Burro Race. Most years, the race course covers 29 miles, following 4x4 dirt roads that wind through alpine meadows up to the barren 13,185-ft Mosquito Pass. No miniature donkey had ever won the world championship. For the majority of the race, Buttercup stuck close or sat in the lead until Marvin missed a course sign, taking them off-route. Running downhill, Buttercup moved like an arrow. Now Marvin had to turn her around. That's when the bucking and kicking started. Buttercup had gone full dragon mode. Now, turned back in the right direction, Buttercup sensed victory.

"She just started sprinting," says Marvin. "I was at the end of the rope, keeping up the best I can. I was on the verge of 'Do I drop this rope?' because I couldn't run any faster. 'Or do I hang on and see what happens?'"

Buttercup moved from fifth to fourth. Then third. Marvin hung on.

"We just passed the guy that was in second place, like he was standing still," remembers Marvin. "We finished and I was like, 'Oh my God, we just won the World Championship.'"

In that rookie season, Buttercup and Marvin would go on to win the men's Triple Crown, taking first place in Leadville and third place in Buena Vista. They returned and won the Men's Triple Crown again in 2020, becoming the team to beat in the world of burro racing.

"Buttercup taught me to go out and get what you want," reflects Marvin. "You finish where you believe you can."

Adapted from reporting by Ashlee Langholz and Cordelia Zars

"We just passed the guy that was in second place, like he was standing still," remembers Marvin. "We finished and I was like, 'Oh my God, we just won the World Championship.'"

THIS PAGE Pack animals, burros enjoy living in herds. Marvin now owns 3 mini donkeys—Buttercup, Peaches and Nugget, pictured here, along with a friend.

UNSEEN BUT FELT

LOCATION	**THE SIERRA NEVADA, CA**
PEOPLE	**FITZ AND BECCA CAHALL**
ACTIVITY	**BACKPACKING, CLIMBING**

ABOVE Camping under the stars in the Sierra Nevada.

Unseen *but Felt*

FITZ CAHALL

The trail disappeared beneath snow. Shielding my eyes from the wind and blinding white powder, I tried to pick a path up through the broad valley. Somewhere beyond lay our exit out of the Sierra. I looked down at my feet, now nestled in 6in of snow. We were nearing the first of two 10,000-ft passes we would need to cross. Behind me, Becca cradled her injured hand close to her heart. With the cold and slippery footing, she'd removed it from the sling and splint in order to keep a glove on it.

UNDER THE WEATHER

Five days earlier, I'd watched as the talus trail Becca was standing on shifted, sending her sliding downhill. An arm outstretched to protect herself, her thumb wound up pinched between sharp rocks, severing a vein and chipping the bone. The emergency room stitches were still fresh. That was day 40 of our trans-Sierra trip. So close to the end of our 300-mile journey, we left the hospital and decided to keep walking, even if we wouldn't be able to climb. Now this.

Heading north out of Tuolumne, the forecast promised perfect weather. A day of showers turned to another day of heavy rain. Sometime in the middle of the night, we felt the temperature plummet. Six years earlier, we'd been a few basins to the north the same week of October when an unforecasted storm dropped 3ft of snow and closed the roads and trails crisscrossing the Sierra. Dozens of hikers had to be plucked from the backcountry via helicopter. Two climbers died of exposure on El Capitan. That storm had been preceded by a heatwave and two days of unsettled weather. Today felt like an echo.

As we hiked past the treeline, I poked at the snow in front of me to interrupt the untouched field of white. Occasionally, the vertigo that comes in whiteout conditions swept over me. Our lightweight gear was meant for summer squalls. It was 28°F and snowing an inch an hour. We needed to move.

It also felt like a personal thesis—you don't have to travel to Pakistan or Baffin Island to have a profound adventure.

LEFT Fifty days in the mountains provided a chance to reflect and thrive.

A MENTAL RESET

Ambitious would be the kind word to describe the climbing trip we'd envisioned. Inefficient, or perhaps stubborn, might better describe the 300-mile course we wove south to north along the crest of California's Range of Light, between the Sierra's famed granite walls. John Muir hiked and climbed across the Sierra over the course of a few weeks, giving rise to the trail that bears his name. Climbing and conservation giant David Brower led a trip in the 1930s, his expedition summiting 55 peaks and concluding with a moonlight ascent of the Matterhorn Peak made famous by Jack Kerouac's *The Dharma Bums*. Admiration of those figures was the inspiration, but it also felt like a personal thesis—you don't have to travel to Pakistan or Baffin Island to have a profound adventure.

It was also an escape. After years of struggling, my career was moving forward at light speed, but demanded what felt like unwavering commitment. I was drinking too much. Not sleeping enough. The specter of depression and burnout tapped at my shoulder. Beyond that, questions hovered over mine and Becca's shared life. Could we ever buy a house? Could we afford to start a family one day? Would it just be simpler to walk away from the creative chaos to get a nine-to-five with steady hours and good health care?

I hoped a heavy pack and 50-ish days in the mountains might serve as a lightning strike of clarity.

LETTING GO

For the first week, a phantom cell phone rang in my pocket. Work filled my dreams. I chased away thoughts that I was shirking my responsibilities. We kept walking. We climbed forgotten routes. We established new ones. For strings of days we saw no one else. We lounged naked on granite slabs after bathing in crystal clear pools. We began to think as one, completing tasks in wordless unison and answering questions the other was about to ask. When cramps and diarrhea wracked Becca's body halfway through, I pulled weight from her bag to help her recover. When a case of stress-induced shingles drained my enthusiasm, Becca quietly fluttered through camp to handle evening chores and organize gear for the next day's climb. Small acts of caring filled the empty spaces of the Sierra.

We kept walking. The phantom cell phone stopped ringing, but after 42 days, I had no obvious marching orders I could take back to the flatlands. So I stopped asking. Our community has a bad habit of labeling this kind of sustained effort and embraced discomfort as suffering. That couldn't be further from the truth. This is thriving. My mind and body loved the rhythm of the rising and setting sun. Sleeping 10 hours a day did not make me a slob. I didn't have to know what day of the week it was to succeed.

I also couldn't stay out here forever.

THUNDER RUMBLED

Lightning struck the ridge above us. The jumbled, snow-covered talus formed a uniform slope obscuring the trail. I took a step forward and slipped. Minutes later Becca tripped in the rocks, ripping the stitches in her hand as she caught herself. When we strayed from the trail, progress slowed. At this rate, we'd spend another night out.

Six weeks of maximal exertion had taken their toll on our bodies. Reality gnawed. It was snowing so hard that it was difficult to open my eyes. Seventeen miles from the nearest road, we were wet from head to foot. The steep slopes provided no flat ground on which to pitch a tent. A blown-out knee or broken ankle would mean leaving the other behind in order to get help. We could stay warm if we just kept moving. We'd navigated by compass in whiteouts before. We'd need to be patient. Steady.

PASSING THE BUCK

Where is the trail?

Poke the snow ahead with a ski pole. Take a step. Boom. Thunder reverberated in my chest. Ski pole prod. Two more steps. A mile takes about 2,500 steps. Many miles to go.

*Where is THE F****** TRAIL?*

The tracks appeared like a gift—the unmistakable footprints of a deer. I followed them. The tracks evaporated 10ft in front of me as if the animal had been plucked from the snow. I looked left, then right, for a shadowy form of a buck. I took a step forward to the place the animal seemed to vanish from. Beneath me, I sensed the uniform ground of the trail we'd lost. We looked at one another in amazement. Each step became more decisive.

When a snowdrift obscured the trail or it switchbacked, the buck's tracks appeared, illuminating the path. Forty-five minutes later, we paused briefly atop the pass to appreciate the force of the wind. The cloud ceiling lifted to offer a momentary glimpse of the path into the next valley and the world of white around us. Not long afterward, we passed the old wooden sign noting the national park boundary. We left Yosemite. Then shivering started. We continued walking.

The day moved forward in the sharp resolution that comes with heightened concentration. I will never forget the booming concussion of lightning strikes as we crossed the second pass, or the detached bemusement of watching Becca covered in rime ice and clinging to tree branches in the steep cliff system we'd accidentally stumbled into. We relied on every tool we'd learned and practiced during a decade of adventure together, but everytime it started to get really bad or we doubted our path, the buck's tracks would appear. We'd follow; its presence unseen, but felt.

LOST AND FOUND

It would be tempting to imbue this moment with deep meaning, but the more I replay that day, the more I believe that to interpret these details as anything other than facts is to deny the moment's beauty. In a blizzard, exposed to lightning and cold, we lost the trail and slowed when we desperately needed to move quickly. Deer tracks appeared when we doubted our way. Sometimes it's just better to believe in a direction rather than questioning the path.

Through the gloom, our exit down Little Slide Canyon appeared. We lurched down 3,000ft of talus, past the snowline into the rain. Knees wavered with exhaustion. We fell repeatedly in the gathering dusk. Too tired to balance across the precarious architecture of slippery logs, we waded thigh-deep through flooded, stinking beaver ponds, and stopped to take our first break in 14 hours as darkness settled. Two miles of flat, wide trail remained. We hugged. Becca took the lead and for the final time of the journey tapped into the unseen reservoir of energy we'd been drinking from liberally on this trip. Too tired to formulate a sentence, I followed, pulled by her slipstream. An hour later, we staggered into a massive campground and wandered lost among the darkened forms of slumbering RVs. Too tired to worry, we quietly set up our tiny tent between two of the metal tubes, smiled at one another, and let a dreamless, calm sleep seep up from wet pine needles and saturated earth.

RIGHT Ridges of golden granite unfold along the crest of the Sierra.

Winter
Vacation

FITZ CAHALL

While Midwesterners embrace the cold, spending an entire winter walking and living in it is a different kind of beast.

LEFT Love at first sight. Emily with Diggins.

Emily Ford never set out to be the first; it just happened to align with her calendar.

Those who live outside of the Upper Midwest don't think of the region as an adventure destination. Those that call it home know that they live in one of the best places on the planet for tapping into nature. The mountains aren't tall, but the landscape spreads out in a series of interconnected lakes, rivers, and trails. In winter, cross-country skiing, dog sledding, and ice climbing provide the hearty with an incredible outlet for adventure. Beauty comes in the form of small connections. Mist rising off of the water on an early fall day. The winter's cold stillness where your heartbeats ring in your ears. An abundance of wildlife.

Emily had already discovered she loved long-distance hiking when she heard about Wisconsin's 1,200-mile-long Ice Age National Scenic Trail. The question wasn't one of desire to hike the trail, but of logistics. From March to December, Emily worked as a gardener at a museum in Duluth, MN. She supplemented her seasonal job by working after-hours in the yards of private clients. It left little free time. When the snow begins to fly in October or November, Emily's work eases, but long-distance hiking in the dead of winter in the Upper Midwest isn't everyone's cup of tea. In fact, it's borderline masochistic.

SCULPTED BY ICE
Hard winters are a way of life in Wisconsin. The average high in January is 28°F with lows dropping to 16°F,

LOCATIONS   **ICE AGE TRAIL, WI**

PEOPLE   **EMILY FORD**

ACTIVITY   **HIKING**

ABOVE Since Diggins was a sled dog, Emily had to make sure he was happy to walk, not run. And to sleep in a tent.

not accounting for windchill. When the north wind brings polar air south, temperatures typically drop to -30°F once or twice a winter. While Midwesterners embrace the cold, spending an entire winter walking and living in it is a different kind of beast. The amount of clothing required to make a trek like that might fill a hallway closet, let alone a backpack. Exertion and cold combined demand more calories, which means more food and a heavier pack.

More than 12,000 years ago, the glacial flows of the last ice age molded and sculpted this landscape. As they retreated, they left behind a subtle but magical topography of long, rolling hills known as "eskers", and thousands upon thousands of small lakes. In 1980,

recognizing the unique nature of the long-distance trail, the US Congress designated the Ice Age Trail as a National Scenic Trail, open to backpacking, snowshoeing, and, in many places, cross-country skiing. The trail follows the outline of the glacier's terminal moraine, or the farthest south the encroaching ice caps made it into what is now the US.

One person, nicknamed Animal by his friends, had pioneered the first winter thru-hike on the Ice Age Trail in 2016. No one was lining up to repeat the feat. Yet, Emily was determined to make the most of her time off. As she researched and formulated a plan, she thought about the possibility of taking a sled dog with her. It would be lonely out there. She'd been dog sledding a

I have my dog. I have my house and everything I need, and I'm surrounded by a world that is allowing me to be a part of it.

few times, and worked part-time at a kennel for a short period. Sled dogs are hearty, love to move, and capable of sleeping out in the worst of conditions. On a whim, she reached out to a Facebook group for Minnesota lady mushers.

"Hey you don't know me, but can I borrow one of your dogs for a 1,200 mile hike in the dead of winter?" laughs Emily. One person responded and said she had the perfect dog.

A few days later, Emily and her partner Flo drove a couple of hours south to meet Cheri Beatty. A small, black, 45-lb sled dog stood out from the pack—Diggins. Diggins was named for Minnesota legend Jessie Diggins, who won the US's first cross-country skiing gold medal in the team sprint with Kikkan Randall.

"As soon as Diggins came over to me, she laid on her back and showed me her belly," remembers Emily. "It was like, 'Okay, let's do this.' It was love at first sight."

Sled dogs run, so Emily took Diggins out on a few warm-up trips to see if she could handle the gentler pace and sleeping in the tent.

On December 28, 2020, Emily and Diggins set off from Potawatomi State Park—at the trail's eastern terminus—and began to follow the ancient lines of glaciers. A group of friends offered words of encouragement as they waved goodbye. Emily hugged Flo, then started walking. She heard the truck pull away, the sound filtering through the skeletal winter trees. Then, a resounding, cold quiet. Her journey had begun.

SETTLING IN
That first week, Emily learned a lot as she settled into the new routine. Realizing she didn't have enough fuel to make both a hot breakfast and dinner, she settled for just one. Many of the summer campgrounds had closed for the season, so she made do with spots in the woods off-trail. Occasionally a local would let her stay in their barn or field. Knee pain overwhelmed her as her body adapted to long days with a heavy pack. When the pain got too much and Emily sat down, Diggins curled between her legs with what felt like support. She limped for 300 miles, but kept walking.

"It was like there was fire just lit under my butt," Emily says. "We got to go. We got to walk home. I wasn't going to give up. This was my trip."

On easier days, she'd call home or post to social media. Soon reporters from local and regional newspapers were calling. People followed along and that's when the gifts started to appear at road crossings and trailheads.

"Socks, hand warmers, candy. People caught wind that I really like Skittles and Starbursts," says Emily.

For Diggins, there was beef jerky and dog treats. After one particularly large snow storm, local snowshoers tramped down unconsolidated snow in advance of her arrival.

As January gave way to February, Emily and Diggins got into a groove. Diggins tolerated Emily's demands to walk instead of run. Emily tolerated Diggins' sniffing

and digging in the snow for roadkill. Even as the trail entered more isolated areas of Wisconsin forest, Emily didn't feel alone. Diggins provided constant friendship and entertainment. The hills grew taller. The snow got deeper. At one point, the new snow developed what backcountry travelers refer to as a "trap crust", where a thin layer of snow on top of the snowpack melts and then quickly refreezes, creating a breakable layer. It might momentarily support a hiker's bodyweight before giving way, sending the hiker knee-deep, even hip-deep in the unconsolidated snow beneath. Progress grew frustratingly slow.

"People ask me, 'Did you ever think about quitting?'" says Emily, before recalling one very difficult section of trap crust. "I think of this moment a lot. I think we were doing a half-mile per hour. I said to Diggs, 'Don't let me stop hiking, ever.' I couldn't think about quitting at the moment. A: It wasn't an option. B: I didn't have phone service at that point. We had to keep going. I had to decide to keep going or sit down and freeze in the snow."

As they headed north and west, the trail grew wilder and more remote. The deciduous trees that define Wisconsin's forests gave way to evergreen hemlocks.

Emily remembers one night setting up camp in a hemlock stand. They'd grown accustomed to the cold, enough that 0°F had begun to feel warm. She dug a tent platform, smoothing the snow to make for more comfortable sleeping. Diggins curled in, one ear listening. To the west, the sunset cast orange light across the white blanket. The moon rose behind them. Emily watched as day gave way to night. An owl hooted in a moonlit forest. In the distance, a rare pack of wolves howled.

"That was the pinnacle of living," remembers Emily. "I have my dog. I have my house and everything I need, and I'm surrounded by a world that is allowing me to be a part of it."

TRAIL'S END
The next morning, they crossed the 1,000 mile mark. Emily scooped Diggins up in triumph. Diggins hated being picked up but sensed this was a special moment. Two hundred more miles of difficult hiking and a thawing snowpack still remained, but Emily felt the pull of the trail's end. On March 5, she set up her last camp at Minnesota's St Croix State Park. To celebrate, her family gathered for dinner to celebrate Emily's and Diggin's achievement. Emily's mom pulled out

firewood. The fire blazed, casting shadows among the trees as Emily feasted on a home-cooked meal, her first in 68 days.

That night, after her family returned to town, Emily felt reality setting in. Diggins spent the last night inside the tent, Emily scratching her head as they fell asleep. Tomorrow, after months together, Diggins would go back to her owner. Emily would return to Duluth. This would be a memory. Emily slept in the next morning, stalling. When she passed through a town she lingered, enjoying a cup of hot chocolate and chatting with people. A few hours later, she and Diggins arrived at Interstate State Park to a line of cars—friends, family, and Cheri, the woman who had loaned Diggins to Emily. The celebration, hugs, and conversation abated and the inevitable came.

"Cheri came over and said, 'I think it's time for Diggins to go home,'" says Emily. "I broke down, like an ugly cry in front of everyone. I didn't care. I remember thinking, 'Don't worry about what people are thinking right now. You have to feel what you're feeling, because it's been a lot. Two and half months.' I just hugged Diggins and said, 'You are the best thing that I could have ever had happen to me on this trip.' I said thank you to Cheri, and she took her and drove home."

THE END IS NEVER EASY
Completing an epic journey sometimes comes with a difficult realization—it can be harder to be back in the comfort of home. The endorphins that come with a day in constant motion go away. Noise and interruptions pour back into an existence accustomed to natural rhythms. Back home, soaking in a hot shower, Emily lost it again. Diggins. The trail.

"I wanted to be back on the trail. Back with Diggins," Emily says. "I wanted to have my true life back, even though I was excited to be home and so thankful for a bed, to be dry, but I wasn't having a very easy time sleeping."

Cheri had extended an offer to let Emily borrow Diggins later that April. Emily took Diggins for a weekend to a cabin in Northern Minnesota. On the trip home, Flo, sensing the growing sadness, suggested Emily talk with Cheri about purchasing Diggins. Good sled dogs are expensive. Finances would be an issue, but Emily texted Cheri. Cheri said she'd check with her family. Emily waited and then a text pinged back.

You know what, you keep Diggins. We feel like you two need to be together and so we want to give her to you.

What had felt like the end just a few weeks earlier had become a new beginning.

Postscript: In March 2021, Emily Ford became the first black person, first woman, first LGBTQ+ person, and the second person ever to complete the Ice Age Trail in winter. Diggins was the first dog to complete the hike in winter.

Adapted from reporting by Ashlee Langholz

The Gimp *Monkeys*

FITZ CAHALL

Heading north on California State Route 41, the road bends right along granite slabs and then dives into the blackness of Wawona Tunnel. At the far end, the emanating pinpoint of light beckons closer and closer. Any climber can sense what's coming. The point grows in size and the car emerges into the California sunshine, while eyes struggle to adapt to the rush of light. And then the heart rates surge and first-timers gasp audibly.

El Capitan's singular form radiates inspiration and intimidation in equal measure, at a volume louder than 11. For a climber, whether or not they climb this granite monolith, this is an aspiration that binds the community together. At one point it was deemed impossible. El Capitan was simply too big, too steep, too difficult. So climbers went to work adapting tactics,

movement, and gear to make it a reality. They matched it with tenacity. A team led by visionary iconoclast Warren Harding succeeded in climbing the first route up the wall in 1959, and after 47 days on the wall—during which they refused rescue from the National Park Service—had established a climbing ethos. That nothing is impossible.

CLIMBERS FIRST

From the tunnel, the road meanders into the pines and open meadows of the valley floor. In El Cap meadow, the undertaking reveals its full scale. Looking up at the 3,000ft of golden granite, the immensity of what climbers Craig Demartino, Pete Davis, and Jarem Frye were about to do hit home. The three friends shared a goal—the first all-adaptive ascent of El Capitan.

LEFT Yosemite's El Capitan was once deemed too big, too steep, and too difficult.

THE GIMP MONKEYS

📍 LOCATION   **YOSEMITE NATIONAL PARK, CA**

PEOPLE   **CRAIG DEMARTINO, PETE DAVIS AND JAREM FRYE**

ACTIVITY   **CLIMBING**

ABOVE Jarem takes a breather on a tiny ledge, gazing over the valley floor hundreds of feet below.

RIGHT Craig leads the climbing trio up El Cap on the lower pitches of Zodiac.

"The right attitude and one arm will beat the wrong attitude and two arms every time."

"All three of us are climbers first, and second, we are disabled," says Craig. "If you're a climber, one of the best things you can do is to climb El Cap. We're not going to raise awareness or to further the cause of disabilities. We are going because we all like to climb."

Jarem lost his leg above the knee to bone cancer at the age of 14. Pete was born without an arm below his elbow. Craig lost his leg after miraculously surviving a 100-ft ground fall after a miscommunication with a belay partner. They coined themselves the Gimp Monkeys, part homage to the Stone Monkeys—a generation of Yosemite climbers who pushed standards and buttons—and as a way of reclaiming a word placed on those living with disabilities.

"It's all about attitude," says Pete. "It's all about perception. What do you really perceive as hard? I feel like having one arm is a pretty minor inconvenience. That's my perception. That's allowed me to do a lot of things in life and not hold me back. The right attitude and one arm will beat the wrong attitude and two arms every time."

A CHANCE TO SHINE
Those looking to make an impact on the sport know that El Capitan is the closest thing climbing has to a Carnegie Hall or Wembley Stadium. In the meadow beneath the 3,000-ft monolith, resting climbers and tourists gather to train binoculars up at the action unfolding above. In a handful of instances, that history resonates so strongly that hordes of television trucks and reporters turn the meadow into a media circus and beam the most famous ascents across the globe.

The trio expected no such coverage, but sensed that the growing adaptive climbing community and broader adventure world would take notice of a successful ascent. At the time, USA Climbing, the body that oversees competitions in the US, hosted several adaptive climbing competitions, but no national championships. Several adaptive climbers had successfully reached the summit of El Cap with non-disabled partners, and the next logical progression in the greater movement for disabled climbers called for an entirely adaptive team.

In June of 2012, the trio shouldered heavy packs and made the tedious approach across talus towards the base of Zodiac. One of El Capitan's classic routes, Zodiac tackles the steep eastern flank of the wall, working its way up through clean corners and overhanging roofs. It's steep enough that in many places, a dropped piece of gear wouldn't touch the wall before it hit ground.

While an elite climber might tackle the route in a very long day, most will spend four or five days working their way up the 16 pitches of climbing. At night, climbers set up portaledges to regroup and sleep before beginning another day of toil. Everything for survival—water, food, extra gear—must be hiked in, hauled up, and hiked out, an exhausting process that is often as physically taxing as the climbing itself.

Sweat, exertion, or an errant movement while hauling heavy bags could compromise the connection between prosthetic and stump, adding a layer of engineering and uncertainty to an ascent. The previous year, Craig and Jarem attempted another route on the western flank of the wall, but were forced to bail after Jarem's prosthetic leg repeatedly fell off. A mechanical failure could easily result in another long, difficult retreat.

The friends tried to leave those questions and uncertainties on the ground. Settling into a steady rhythm, Pete and Craig swapped leads and hauled the gear as Jarem followed behind, jugging up the rope with ascenders. In the evening, warm air rushing upward carried scraps of laughter and the clinking of climbing gear being organized. Down in the valley, the Yosemite faithful took note via binoculars and telescopes. Cell coverage and Instagram had yet to arrive on the side of El Cap.

ON THE WALL
Morning light spilled over the shoulder of Half Dome as the friends awoke, each handling a set of chores to efficiently break down the night's camp, before making steady progress up the wall. The occasional falls and tangled ropes added highlights to the memory rather than threatening to derail their goal. Each day they climbed into the fading light, before pausing to assemble their hanging camp of portaledges. A full moon appeared, its soft light reflecting off the granite and replacing any need for a headlamp. The sun rose and set three times as the trio stayed focused on what lay ahead.

They navigated through the route's distinct cruxes—the Black Tower, the Mark of Zorro, and the Nipple. Pete packed away his prosthetic arm and deftly used his stump to balance on small holds on the hardest pitches. Jarem doggedly ascended. Craig supplied a steady stream of optimism when things got momentarily difficult. For their efforts, they basked in life on the wall. Swifts danced on updrafts feet from the cliff, their wings whispering. The joy of water after a long pitch in the sun. The outrageous sense of freedom that comes from

sitting on a portaledge, back resting against the wall, imagining yourself in a tiny craft on a sea of granite.

Soon the summit felt closer than the ground. Confidence billowed like a sail, alleviating the gathering exhaustion. A hundred feet below the edge of El Cap, Pete took the lead one more time, navigating through a final roof before grabbing the lip and manteling onto flat ground in a tangle of gear the way so many climbers had before. It was both remarkable and recognizable. Jarem and Craig each made their way to join Pete.

"I have never been this worked in my entire life," Jarem shared. "Most painful, most difficult, most incredible thing I've ever done."

Hugs exchanged and smiling ear to ear, the trio took a moment to bask in what they'd achieved. A small group of friends had hiked up to celebrate. Pete sipped a beer as he relished life back on horizontal ground.

"Finishing up the last pitch, I mentally was kind of over it, but there was never a point where I thought that we weren't going to do this," said Pete. "Took us four nights. Five days. Not the speed ascent, but slow and steady wins the race. And this being the first all disabled ascent, I expected that, but we got it done."

Sports and communities evolve incrementally. The horizon always shifts. The next generation is already chasing it. Sometimes history simply looks like three friends, an idea, and the hard work to make it happen. That's the thruline from Warren Harding's first ascent in 1959 to Craig, Pete, and Jarem's all-adaptive ascent of El Cap in 2012. Call something impossible, and a climber will be there to figure out how to make it possible.

Postscript: Two years afterward, USA Climbing organized the first Paraclimbing National Championship. Craig would go on to compete and podium at the second and third Paraclimbing World Cups with a global set of competitors, becoming one of the first professional climbers from the adaptive community. Today, most major outdoor brands support adaptive athletes. There are half-a-dozen organizations supporting adaptive climbing athletes in America, with regular meetups, trips, and gatherings. Chapters have sprung up in major cities, with many climbing gyms recognizing the role they can play to expand access and build community. A new generation of climbers is pushing for paraclimbing to be included in the 2028 Summer Paralympics in Los Angeles.

The Fear *Is Real*

FITZ CAHALL

A can of bear spray slung over her shoulder, the .44 magnum on her hip, and with hundreds of miles behind her, she found her resolve.

Kat Cannell clicked on the YouTube link. On screen, the outdoor equivalent of a horror movie unfolded in front of her.

"I just had a grizzly with two cubs come at me and she got my head good," the hunter calmly said into the camera. With a broken arm and wounds on his head, arm, and shoulder, he is covered in blood. "I don't know what's under my hat, my ear, my arm, pieces of stuff hanging."

BEAR NECESSITIES

The video started circulating in October 2016, two weeks before Kat was set to embark on a 350-mile horse-packing journey from her home in Ketchum, ID, to Chico Hot Springs, just north of Yellowstone National Park in Montana. The YouTube incident occurred right off her intended route.

The nexus of Idaho, Montana, and Wyoming remains one of the wildest and most intact ecosystems in the lower 48. Nature takes center stage in Yellowstone, where tourists flock to catch glimpses of bison, moose, elk, and black bear. Away from the RVs and tourist flocks, Mother Nature goes about her business with little regard for humans. At the top of the food chain sits *Ursus arctos horribilis*—better known as the grizzly bear. While bears often own oversized real estate in many people's minds, the Northern Rockies' grizzly population demands serious respect. Given the season and migratory patterns, Kat's journey would put her right in the crosshairs.

LOCATIONS   **ROCKY MOUNTAINS, ID, MO**

PEOPLE   **KAT CANNELL**

ACTIVITY   **HORSE-PACKING**

ABOVE The Tom Miner Basin is home to 20 grizzlies year-round, but as many as 40 in the late summer and fall.

THIS PAGE Another morning start for Kat and her horses as they make the journey from Idaho to Montana.

"I'm sitting there watching this video like, 'Okay, Kat, you are nuts. You're absolutely nuts. This is stupid,'" she remembers.

THE FEAR FACTOR

Loosely speaking, fear falls into two groups—extrinsic and intrinsic. The former fears are rational. Rockfall in loose granite gulleys. Touchy avalanche conditions on backcountry ski days. Summer lightning storms in the alpine peaks. Grizzly bears in the Northern Rockies at treeline just before hibernation in October certainly qualify. While we may underestimate or overestimate the likelihood of their occurrence, we've developed systems that mitigate the odds of something bad happening. No outcome is guaranteed, but through tactics and planning we can aim for "safe-ish".

The intrinsic fears are harder to manage and every bit as powerful.

For much of her life, those fears haunted Kat: "Fear of not being pretty enough. Fear of not being successful. Fear of not being a good enough person." She grew up a self-described "horse girl" on a working ranch in Idaho's majestic Sawtooth Mountains. As soon as she could walk she was wandering the pastures among her father's

comes a fear that others will notice these perceived flaws. Often, people dealing with the condition isolate themselves from friends and family. Many turn to substance abuse as a coping mechanism.

"In college, I ended up in rehab for bulimia, anorexia, drinking, and self-harm," remembers Kat. "I came out a healthier person, but that being said, it doesn't just go away. You still struggle."

As she struggled, Kat turned to a childhood idea. In their barn, a Decker pack saddle hung on the wall. With it, a rider and horse team can carry enough to travel long distances. She was six years into recovery, still occasionally fighting through waves of internal fear over her appearance.

"I remember scraping myself off and saying 'This is bullshit. This is not going to be me anymore.' At that moment, I just wanted to be an adventurer and wanted to do something badass."

TOOLING UP
In the spring of 2016, she embarked on a 620-mile ride from Hailey, ID, to Sierraville, CA. That fall, she set her mind on the shorter, but arguably more challenging, Idaho to Montana trip—via seven mountain passes in the heart of bear country. She gathered as much information as possible from the horse packing community. She sought advice from locals on how to manage the possibility of encountering a grizzly. An early season blizzard complicated matters—and then came the grizzly attack video.

"This was something that I was really passionate about, so I didn't want to give up because of fear," Kat says. "Blindly charging forward wasn't the right move either, so I strategized."

Her first line of defense were the horses. A human becomes bigger and more intimidating on horseback. Second line—noise. Most attacks occur when a bear is surprised at close range. She draped two big cowbells around the necks of her horses and buffered that with a playlist of favorite songs she could sing along to.

Should those not work and a bear charged, bear spray was the next option. Finally, her husband gifted her a .44 magnum, the ridiculously large revolver made famous by Clint Eastwood's *Dirty Harry* movies. Should it come to life and death, a large caliber bullet has a chance of penetrating a bear's skull.

horses. In high school, she competed in barrel racing—a rodeo event where rider and horse complete a clover leaf pattern in the fastest time possible. She guided horseback rides in Bozeman, MT. She was a strong, capable athlete and outdoorswoman, and yet since fourth grade Kat had struggled with a condition called body dysmorphia.

"It's like hyper exaggerating your flaws to the point where someone who is size zero might look in the mirror and see themselves as a size 15," Kat says.

A person's perspective on their body twists the way a funhouse mirror might distort a reflection. With it

PASSING TIME

Of the seven passes on her itinerary, two stood out as question marks—Patterson Pass and Buffalo Horn Pass. Enough snow, washouts or downed trees and the slender single-track trails that crest them could be impassable on horseback. Five days in, she crossed through the abandoned mining town of Patterson, its decrepit shacks adding to the intimidating ambience. That afternoon, hunters warned her that they'd seen a big grizzly and that the trail was covered in snow. Kat slept fitfully in a light tent, but awoke determined to at least try.

Dawn broke perfectly and Kat and her horse team worked up 3,000ft of snow-covered scree slopes to Patterson Pass, surrounded by an expanse of rocky peaks. Snowdrifts reached to her horses' stomachs, but Kat continued on toward Montana. For the next 10 days, she crested ranges and crossed the big open country that defines the American West as she worked her way to the final test of Buffalo Horn Pass in the Gallatin mountains.

Kat peppered the locals with questions. That's when she began to hear about Tom Miner Basin, a broad valley with rolling hills peppered with sagebrush and evergreens, just beyond the pass. Though the area is home to 20 year-round resident grizzlies, in the late summer and fall the population often swells to 40 grizzlies roaming through the browning grass. Most of the people she connected with advised her against this final leg of her journey.

"Too dangerous. Too much snow. Too many bears," they told her.

Yet over the course of 18 days and 300 miles, a quiet confidence had grown inside Kat.

INTO THE BASIN

"I know why I'm here," Kat said to herself the night before she reached Tom Miner. "I'm here because I need to overcome the fears society has instilled into me. I need to not be afraid of everything in life, whether it's not being attractive enough or afraid of social situations, or afraid I'm not making enough money or afraid of going over a path with grizzly bears. Life is about ignoring your fears and going forth with confidence. That's what I'm going to do tomorrow."

On the cold November morning, Kat packed up camp, saddled her horses, and started up the snowy trail. She passed three other riders, heading down, who told her she was crazy.

"It was the closest I got that whole trip to turning around," she recalls.

A can of bear spray slung over her shoulder, the .44 magnum on her hip, and with hundreds of miles behind her, she found her resolve. She needed one last tool to pull her and her horses up and over the pass into Tom Miner Basin. She hit play and started singing.

Hey Jude… John, Paul, George, and Ringo sang in her ears. The cowbells clanged. Kat sang along. "I started singing. My voice was trembling. I was shaking," remembers Kat. "I saw these huge wolf tracks coming down the trail."

In the fresh snow, Kat could see the wolf had turned off the trail.

"Okay, my singing voice is working. My cowbells are loud enough. They know we are coming."

The words carried over the new snow into the quiet of the open forest. Louder and louder. Slightly off key, but powerfully sung, they sounded like determination. Then the grizzly tracks appeared. They too veered abruptly from the trail to escape the cacophony of someone learning to believe in themselves.

"It was done. It was over. There was nothing else to be worried about."

Kat sang louder, straight on through Tom Miner Basin, parting the sea of unseen grizzly bears, her voice growing more confident as she rode the final miles towards Chico Hot Springs.

"I could go 50,000 miles on a horse and still look like me. There's not going to be some holy transformation. I truly feel more confident about walking through life as this five-foot-eight girl who's 165 lbs," says Kat. "I didn't need to change how I looked. I just needed to change how I looked at myself."

Adapted from reporting by Jen Altschul

I just wanted to be an adventurer and wanted to do something badass.

THIS PAGE Tom Miner Creek Road, leading to bear country.

PREVIOUS SPREAD Looking back toward Buffalo Horn Pass, MT.

BANANAS AND PEANUT BUTTER

LOCATION	**CONTINENTAL DIVIDE**
PEOPLE	**QUINN BRETT**
ACTIVITY	**HANDCYCLING**

ABOVE Quinn's e-assist handcycle brought a sense of freedom back to her life.

Bananas
and Peanut Butter

QUINN BRETT

The Continental Divide separates the water that runs toward the Pacific Ocean from the water that runs toward the Atlantic, Arctic Ocean, and the Gulf of Mexico. Starting in Cape Prince of Wales in western Alaska, it runs through western Canada into the United States along the Rocky Mountains, then through the Sierra Madre Occidental mountains into Mexico. That water touches everyone in western North America.

The Great Divide Mountain Bike route extends from Banff, Canada, bobbing and weaving over the Continental Divide nearly 30 times, unfurling 2,745 miles to the south following mostly Forest Service roads to Antelope Wells in New Mexico. In biking culture, it is the birthplace of bikepacking. I first heard about it from my friend Justin and the route had intrigued me the way any giant endurance challenge would.

I have been an extreme endurance athlete for most of my adult life, as both a professional climber and working as a climbing ranger in Rocky Mountain National Park. Since my late 20s, life revolved around adventure, from putting up first ascents in Patagonia and Greenland, to running long distances across Zion National Park and the Grand Canyon. In summer, I roamed high alpine peaks before the fall sent me farther west to Yosemite and Zion. I traveled abroad in the winter, before finding my way back to the desert to soak up some warmth.

That all changed in October of 2017 when I fell while climbing in Yosemite National Park on the Nose of El Capitan. Climbers take falls all the time, but this was different. I fell over a hundred feet. Somehow, I am still here with a brain that is mostly intact, but I broke my

back, causing injury to my spinal cord. I am now paralyzed from the waist down.

The injury consumed me, both physically and emotionally as I explored the world anew, in a body that no longer responded to my physical commands. Everything from driving a car, to going to the bathroom, to putting on pants, required a whole new set of skills. I was forced to peel away the layers of self, developing my communication skills as I spoke my needs to others, even as I tried to understand them myself.

My drive to explore the outside world did not diminish because of my injury. Sure, one could say that my thirst for adventure may have led to my injury, but it would now be the source of my recovery.

RETURN TO SANITY

I spent six weeks in intensive care and in-patient recovery, and another six weeks at a spinal cord injury rehab hospital in Denver. I spent a few more months living in the city at a friend's house, doing out-patient rehab. During this time, Justin held a fundraiser in Estes Park, CO, to purchase an off-road hand cycle. Imagine a three-wheeled recumbent bike, but instead of leaning back, my body's in a kneeling position. I lean forward on my chest, my hands alternating

I might be sitting in a wheelchair, but I am not sitting still.

between grabbing a normal-looking mountain bike handlebar and turning a hand-crank—like pedals but for my arms. The position depends on the terrain, balance, and whether I'm cranking up a hill or zooming down one. Cycling with your arms is different from cycling with your legs, which have much bigger muscles.

When I returned to trails, some that had been a quick 20-minute run prior to my injury, now took 20 minutes for just the first half-mile on the hand cycle. My arms alone, without e-assist, struggled to gain momentum on the steep uphills, or with navigating too much side-hill for the three-wheels, meaning I was very susceptible to tipping over. Tight trees or big boulders narrowed the trail so I couldn't go any farther. These first few forays left me defeated and physically exhausted. I needed to use my arms for all my other daily activities—pushing around the house, showering, and getting in and out of the car.

Though I had initially refused the option of e-assist for the bike, a few months battling the terrain put my ego in check. I purchased a battery and e-assist motor for the crank. Life, terrain, and happiness re-opened!

I started going on longer and longer bike rides, learning the ins and outs of the hand cycle, riding around Rocky Mountain National Park, and even up to the Boulder Field on Longs Peak. What a joy it was to return to the places where I spent so much of my time freely exploring. Out on the trails the idea of biking from Banff to New Mexico sprouted in my mind, and I started prepping. In quintessential style, I marked out

OPPOSITE PAGE Quinn averaged 100 miles per day throughout the 25-day journey.

ABOVE Joe, Quinn, and Brody Leven pedaling through a long stretch of dirt road in rural Montana.

PREVIOUS SPREAD
Most of the Tour Divide is made up of dirt roads that climb and wind their way through forests, mountains, and deserts.

LEFT Joe contemplates the wisdom in eating multiple servings of ice cream with another 30 miles still to ride.

BELOW LEFT A hug and a back stretch from Robert Prechtl.

BELOW RIGHT Quinn taking in the eclectic amenities in Pie Town, New Mexico.

RIGHT Joe at sunset in Montana as the first thunderstorm of the trip lurks in the background.

four weeks in June and July of 2021. It had been three and a half years since I had experienced the simple joys of planning, logistics, and being excited about something.

I looked at maps, gleaning information from Justin and reading trip reports. I calculated that I needed to ride about 100 miles a day to complete the endeavor, given the amount of time I could take off from work. I also needed to figure out the logistics. What was I—and what were the batteries—capable of? I ordered four more 9.5-lb batteries, shoving them into the bike's panniers.

I tried my systems out on the 100-mile White Rim trail in Moab, UT. After a successful day of riding, the Great Divide seemed within reach. Now, I just needed to string nearly a month of 100-mile days together.

FRIENDS MAKE IT BETTER
It's in the spirit of the Great Divide route to ride unsupported. Ultimately, I knew I couldn't abide by that fully because I needed to charge my batteries and

stay on a tight time frame. I also wanted to have my wheelchair for the end of each day. Changing seating positions is essential to avoid pressure sores, a grave side effect of spinal cord injury. I also didn't want to be piggybacked into hotels, restaurants, or bathrooms. My best version of being unsupported and as independent as possible during the endeavor required a support team to follow along, managing the solar-powered, portable charging stations to keep the batteries primed for a daily rotation.

For some stretches, you can plan on a town with a hotel every 100 miles. Conversely, other stretches landed us at campgrounds or undesignated sites on public land. I dove into a spreadsheet, mapping and reserving hotels and campgrounds as necessary—calling hotels directly to ensure the availability of disability accommodations, like a roll-in shower with a bench.

I also desired an adventure buddy. Enter Joe Foster. We met at a Paralympic Nordic skiing event in Breckenridge,

CO, and hit it off. An able-bodied human who has accumulated a long list of big adventures, Joe's familiar with the added daily tasks and secondary health considerations that come with a spinal cord injury. And he was between jobs, making him the perfect candidate. I asked. He said, "Hell yes!"

"When Quinn started talking to me about the Great Divide, I did not think of what we would have to change because of her injury," remembers Joe. "It was kind of just like, 'Oh, you want to spend a month bikepacking and riding singletrack? Yeah, let's go do it!'"

REKINDLED SPIRIT

We arrived in Eureka, MT, about 30 miles south of the border, at the house of my friend Jason, who I met while we both rehabbed at Craig Hospital. Since the border was closed in 2021 and we couldn't begin in Banff, we used his home as a base to finish the last bit of planning, and for quick access to our launch point. Jason also had an adaptive bike, and joined us for half the day.

The first few days were grueling, as a heat wave swept over Montana. Thankfully, the abundance of rivers and lakes meant we could jump in or soak a shirt. Joe hung with me and my blatant regiment for hammering out relatively big distances, averaging 100 miles and eight to 12 hours on our bikes each day. As the heat subsided, we got into a groove. We set the alarm for 5.30 a.m. and would be on the bike between 6.30 a.m. and 8am. Our days were simple. Get up, eat, go to the bathroom, get on the bikes, pee, eat, water splash, bike some more, eat, pee, arrive at camp, eat, help where we can, sleep, and repeat.

The most significant challenges came when we stopped pedaling. In the outdoor environment, I have my systems for camping, using the bathroom, and navigating terrain dialed. I move with a freedom that I don't have in the built environment that supposedly has laws to create equitable access for people with disabilities. Yet, it is distinctly confining —sidewalks lacking curb cuts along the street, restaurants with steps, and hotels without accessible accommodations. Where to eat, use the bathroom, and shower?

Days turned into weeks and our bodies adapted to the routine. By the end of the first week, we made it to the Teton range in Wyoming. On schedule, we spun out miles through the state and into Colorado.

By the end of the third week, we arrived in New Mexico. Though the end was in sight, it still felt like anything could go wrong. Because my bike has so many moving parts, a motor or battery could easily fail. One of us could still get injured. Similar to climbing El Capitan in a day, reality doesn't sink in until you're on the last pitch. It wasn't until the very last day—nay the last 30 miles—that I let myself feel the gravitas of what we'd achieved. "It's here!" I exclaimed. "We're doing it!"

From meadows filled with tiny red flowers to waves of mosquitoes, amiable strangers, and a few all-day downpours, with abhorrent mud that sticks to your drive train, the trip was perfect. We filled the days with challenge and joy. I slept better than I'd ever slept since my injury. I felt tired and my brain chatter finally quieted to a whisper. Before my injury, bananas and peanut butter were my go-to foods, but I hadn't craved that at all since. On the trip, I devoured them again.

On the 25th day of our tour, having pedaled over 2,500 miles, accompanied by Joe, my mom, Justin, and my friends Robbie and Andy (the latter who were providing support along the way), I rolled into Antelope Wells, NM.

This injury may have quieted my lower half and my limbs, and battered my confidence and self-identify— but it did not quiet my drive to move, to explore, to connect with the earth. Preparing for the Great Divide wasn't just about logistics. It was also about healing.

I might be sitting in a wheelchair, but I am not sitting still. I would rather be out on my trike than staring at a computer or idling at home. I might be physically disabled—and I might be more capable and equipped for the world then I ever would have been otherwise. I'm a semblance of me again.

Though the end was in sight, it still felt like anything could go wrong.

Chapter Three
Peaks and Valleys

Transitions

FITZ CAHALL

The Dog Leg Chute is a short skin from Crystal Mountain's groomed runs. When two skiers arc interlacing turns down the 20-ft wide chute, bordered by rock walls, it reminds me of the double helixed strands of DNA. The line always puts a smile on my face, but the approach up the backside of this small peak always warrants thoughtful conversation about avalanche conditions. Winds blowing over the crest of the Washington Cascades push snow into an open bowl. Cornices appear overhead like frozen waves. At its steepest, the slope angle increases to 45 degrees— textbook avalanche start zone.

Becca and I carefully traversed the slope one at a time, regrouping in a safe spot before digging with gloved hands into the powder to look for the weak layers that signal dangerous conditions. The last, steep 30ft demanded the most care. I crossed tentatively before reaching the safety of the ridge. Becca followed my track, but with steps to go, a small slab no bigger than

a dining room table broke beneath her, pulling her feet away. In desperation, she grabbed a small tree and hung on as the slide entrained snow below, sweeping over our skin track 230ft below.

We collected ourselves on the slender ridge. To one side was the slope we'd just escaped. On the other, our intended descent line down the Dog Leg. A few feet above us, the flat summit tempted us with the ease of transitioning our skis and snowboard from uphill to downhill mode. But after the near miss, our current perch seemed like an appropriate place to head down.

With the edge of my snowboard, I carved a small, flat platform into the 45-degree slope. Becca carefully removed the climbing skins from the base of her skis and gingerly stepped into her bindings, before making room for me. I assembled my splitboard, stepped up to the ridgecrest, then dug the board's edge into the snow. I put one foot in, buckled, and then took a deep breath

TRANSITIONS

LOCATIONS **CRYSTAL MOUNTAIN, WA**

PEOPLE **FITZ AND BECCA CAHALL**

ACTIVITY **SKIING, SNOWBOARDING**

ABOVE Exploring the backcountry near Crystal Mountain.

THIS PAGE Once you take the leap, there's no way back, just down.

as I lifted my other foot off the snow. Balanced on one foot with the mountain falling steeply away on either side, time slowed. A misstep would lead to a tumbling fall down the mountain. I'd done this hundreds of times but never with the same consequences. For an instant, I became deeply aware of all the tiny muscles in my core firing, struggling to keep this moment of balance intact. My foot landed perfectly in the binding. Clipped in, I balanced on the ridge as Becca disappeared into a graceful blur of whispering snow and gravity.

SIMPLER TIMES

Eight years earlier, Becca and I started exploring the myriad of forested slopes and peaks that existed beyond the boundaries of Tahoe's Disneyland-esque ski resorts. Ahead of me, Becca would stride evenly upward on skis equipped with climbing skins. I would wallow behind her on snowshoes, my snowboard strapped to my back, lumbering in a sweaty mess to find Becca patiently waiting on the summit. I would scatter the contents of my backpack and snowshoes across a small snow platform, watch, and then curse as the wind tugged an empty granola bar wrapper from my open pack into the ridge tops' circular wind currents. These transitions

were a haphazard panoply of buckle snaps and re-organization that I completed with bare hands. Then, I'd warm my hands, change into a dry set of gloves, collapse my ski poles, and find some spare spot on my pack to clip them to. I'd stammer apologies as Becca tugged the skins from the bottom of her skis, folded them cleverly around her forearm, and shoved them neatly into a small opening in her pack. She loved me anyway.

When splitboards evolved into aggressive downhill machines, I happily ditched my snowshoes and vowed that no skier would ever have to wait for me on a summit. I practiced and began to take pride in the process of transitioning from uphill to downhill. Summit. Unclip. Peel back climbing skins. Pull out the hat tucked into my breast pocket. Carefully convert the splitboard from skis to single plank. Secure bindings. Haste was the enemy. A relaxed but efficient method bound in muscle memory. Becca no longer had to wait. I took a certain amount of nerdish pride in that.

AN ESCAPE HATCH

Becca and I evolved as partners and individuals. There were no discussions or lightning bolt moments, but we

RIGHT Snow tracks in perfect unison.

felt the quiet shift in unison. We moved to Seattle and our lives thrived. We'd found a working balance between our competing desires of professionalism and mountain exploits. We felt the support of friends and family like granite bedrock. A half-dozen of us would pile into our friend's battered, early 1990s Chevy Astro Van at 5.30 a.m. and drive two hours to backcountry stashes. Days sped by in a blur of exertion, conversation, laughter, and snow. One December day, returning from the Cascades, Becca and I stopped at a U-Cut Christmas tree farm before decorating it with strung-together popcorn and cranberries, and old ski passes as ornaments. Seattle had become home.

We understood that, as we evolved, so would the constraints on our time. We valued being in the mountains together, but we didn't want to drive two hours back and forth, three times a week. A cozy weekend cabin was a hallucinatory daydream. Instead, I bought a 13-ft, 1976 fiberglass Scamp travel trailer designed to be pulled by a car. The brand name seemed fitting. It cost me a little less than a month's rent. There was a reason. Inside, mold grew on walls behind rotting wood cabinets. The electrical system was completely fried. Rust clung to any metal elements. I set to work.

Atop a ridge, I make eye contact with Becca and promise, as I have a hundred times before, "I've got you."

I took it to its bones, scrubbed with bleach, sanded fiberglass cabinets, patched holes, tore out tangles of wiring, and electrocuted myself only once. I wired in a stereo. Our next-door neighbors poked their heads in to find me clad in safety goggles, fiberglass dust, and a respirator. I was building something—something more than a refurbished 1976 travel trailer. I was creating a path back to the mountains, to those days in Tahoe when a glance out the window was the only forecast I needed. I was cutting out excess transition time between the snow and our Seattle home. By staying up there, we could halve the total driving time.

For eight-and-a-half months, I'd wander to the driveway after dinner and work. I had a new motivation now. I was about to become a father.

I'd heard the stern warnings delivered from new parents:

"Life is going to change."

"You will never be able to ski or climb."

"It's impossible to get out of the house."

Every time I got an unsolicited warning of doom about how my life was going to be one giant suckfest of diapers and 4am feedings, I reflected on the role models I'd met over the years. Roger and Merridy skied twice as many days a year as me, and they had a two-year-old. Craig was as good a father as he is a climber, which said a lot for his capabilities in both endeavors. Siri ran a 40-acre vegetable farm with a child strapped to her back. Steve had five kids, a seamless unit of outdoor loving joy. I offset my nervousness with the knowledge that I'd built our escape hatch into the mountains. It was sitting in the driveway.

★★★

On a warm fall night, I took a break from applying what felt like the fifteenth layer of paint on the fiberglass interior and sat on the front step of the trailer while I sipped a beer. Light from the now-functional dome lamp leaked into the darkness of the driveway.

I remembered that day in the Crystal backcountry. I stood balanced on the edge of the intellectual equivalent of that slender ridge. One foot in. One foot out. Teetering or balanced? No way to ride back down the way I climbed up—only the path forward. The tenuous moment of transition.

"Believe in your vision. Embrace the work that vision requires," I said to myself.

In the November darkness on a Seattle side street, I closed my eyes and imagined what I wanted to see.

When the snow flies, there's an extra bag to pack. Becca and I sit three-deep with our child on the bench seat of the old Toyota truck as we navigate an awkward trailer through Friday traffic. We pull into Crystal's parking lot to curl into a ball of three on the snug table-turned-bed and let our breath heat the small trailer while the collecting snow insulates us from above. The interior lights cast dimly into the gathering flakes. Coffee brews on the stove. As flakes collect on eyelashes, we watch as our child feels the first cold kiss of snow. Maybe one day they will want their mother to teach them to ski. Maybe not. At the very least, they will know how to make a decent snowball.

Atop a ridge, I make eye contact with Becca and promise, as I have a hundred times before, "I've got you." She snaps her skis into the fall line, drops off the cornice, and leads us into parenthood. At the bottom, we turned and looked back at two interlaced tracks. Two signatures etched with flourish down a slender swath of snow spelling out our vision for a life ahead.

Postscript: On December 21, 2011, the first day of winter, Becca gave birth to our first son, Teplin. A decade on, we remain regulars in Crystal Mountain's B-Lot. Today, both Teplin and his brother Wiley ski faster than their parents and excel at the art of snowball making. Traffic has only gotten worse, but our weekend treks to the mountain have never felt more vital.

Sacred *Slopes*

LEN NECEFER

These mountains, in all their harshness, are also balanced by a sentiment of healing. Maybe they would take pity on me for simply trying.

Porous black volcanic rocks covered in snow and an icy rime cracked beneath each step. Winds funneled up through the gullied ridges to our left, forcing us off the ridge and onto the corniced snow to our right. Our skis and splitboards acted as sails, fluttering our packs and bodies with each gust. As we ascended farther the temperature dropped precipitously. The gusts turned into sustained gale-force winds, and my breathing became increasingly labored as it got harder and harder to inhale. Numbness wrapped around my hands. I looked down and clenched them into fists in my gloves to see how the feeling would change. Not too long ago, I had glimpsed the silhouette of Connor Ryan, barely discernible in the distance, cresting a ridge. Now, as I scanned the

landscape, his figure had vanished, consumed either by the summit or the shrouding clouds. It was a stark reminder of our miniscule existence in the vast wilderness. I had to remind myself that this was Arizona, and we were on our sacred mountain.

I arrived at the summit a few minutes after Connor and Forrest Shearer. The snow and the clouds seamlessly blended into a single shade of white interspersed by the black volcanic rocks. Without these markers it was nearly impossible to know where the ground was before us. Forrest sat behind a rock blind sheltering from the wind as Connor placed tobacco and sang songs from his ceremony to thank the mountain.

SACRED SLOPES

📍 LOCATIONS	**DOOK'O'OOSŁÍÍD, AZ**
PEOPLE	**LEN NECEFER, CONNOR RYAN, FORREST SHEARER**
ACTIVITY	**HIKING, SKIING, SPLITBOARDING**

ABOVE Forrest floating down Dook'o'oosłííd.

In Navajo we reference our six sacred mountains in nearly every religious ceremony, but we also reference four sacred rivers that emanate from these snowpacks through the phrase, "Tó ei Iina"—water is life". Anderson Hoskie, a Navajo medicine man we had visited the day before our summit, told me to listen to the songs I had recorded of him singing, and to try to sing along when I reached the summit. The words of the Navajo mountain songs felt foreign. The wind gusts muffled the speaker on my phone. I kept missing words, and my pitch seemed an octave too low. I thought about how many other people carried these words with them; I wondered how many carried them up this mountain, and if they also struggled like I did. These mountains, in all their harshness, are also balanced by a sentiment of healing. Maybe they would take pity on me for simply trying.

CLICKING IN

A few years ago, I would have scoffed at the idea of a Navajo person using snow sports to tell a story about a sacred mountain. For the better part of my teens and 20s I refused to learn how to ski, even when presented with the opportunity, in large part because of the controversy around this massif. Growing up, I

remember hearing in my community about how sewage was going to be used to make artificial snow at a ski resort on one of our sacred mountains, Dook'o'oosłííd, near Flagstaff, AZ. I watched Native protesters chain themselves to bulldozers on the opening day of the resort, and I remember the heavy-handed deployment of police to arrest organizers. To participate in a sport desecrating a sacred space conflicted with the teachings I had been raised with as a Navajo person—an ethic of protecting these places for those coming after me.

After a career change that brought me to Colorado in 2015, I began climbing each of the sacred mountains during the snow-free months, following the clockwise pattern they are referenced in ceremony. I met Forrest, a professional snowboarder and climate activist, in shared activism around the Bears Ears National Monument in southern Utah in the fall of 2016. Forrest has spent much of his life adventuring in high alpine environments and has seen the impacts of climate change firsthand. In our conversations about sacred mountains and climate change, we often spoke about an urgency to see and experience these places before they are irreparably changed. That first winter in Colorado I decided to teach myself how to ski, and with the support of Forrest and others I decided to push myself further with this new skill to explore these regions.

In December 2018, at Colorado's Berthoud Pass, I met Connor, a young Lakota man inspired to turn professional skier after his transformative Hambleycha, a vision quest ceremony demanding solitude and deprivation in a sweat lodge to seek life's direction. Connor had emerged from it with a haunting question—"What if I'm the last skier?"— The answer appeared simple: he did not want to be the last skier, and his path forward would be to do everything he could to ensure this sport could be passed on. Over the next few months, Connor and I began sharing longer walks on our skis in the Colorado Front Range. It seemed, however, that we had to travel farther and to more remote reaches of these peaks to find a consistent snowpack.

Connor, Forrest, and I shared a similar mindset that enveloped culture and connection to mountain landscapes. When we set off to the western sacred mountain, Dook'o'oosłííd, we hoped to fortify that link

for ourselves, and our communities, even in the face of a changing climate.

STORIES WRITTEN INTO LANDSCAPES

The identities of many Indigenous cultures are woven together by language, sacred histories, and ceremonial cycles, embedded within a broader landscape that fosters their vibrance. The traditional names of these mountains already serve as a reminder of how much they have changed in the past century. The Navajo Dook'o'oosłííd—and its Hopi name, Nuva'tukya'ovi —roughly translate to "the peak that does not melt", referencing a year-round snowcap which no longer exists. For the 13 tribes that call Northern Arizona home, the ecosystems and cultural traditions that depend upon snowpacks and snowmelt are also uncertain.

While many of the beliefs of these tribes about the mountain differ, there are commonalities—that the water, soil, plants, and animals from this mountain have inalienable spiritual and medicinal properties; that the peaks represent living beings and are home to deities; and that the tribes and its members have a duty to

OPPOSITE PAGE The stunning sacred Navajo country.

THIS PAGE Connor makes an offering of tobacco on top of Dook'o'oosłííd.

protect them. The loss of snow will inevitably mean impacts on the ceremonial cycles, languages, and sacred history that these tribes steward. I have seen firsthand how certain medicinal plants are harder to find, often moving farther up slopes to find cooler temperatures on the mountain, and in some instances running out of elevation to gain, forcing me and my relatives to travel north to other mountain ranges.

In ceremonies, I saw the power of these mountains to heal; in my own mountain adventures I saw their power to end life. My attempt to karaoke our traditional songs in the high alpine felt like a balance between these realities—one of reverence and also taking humility in my challenged efforts in continuing these traditions. The story of the Navajo people is written into these landscapes and we are reminded in our songs of this connection. However, this story felt incomplete for me until I connected my own path into the stories held in these places. I become another link in the chain of human memory of this place as these stories continue to exist both within ourselves and these landscapes.

The gap created by decades of policy to remove us physically and psychologically from our sacred lands requires us to write this new chapter: one free of violence and dispossession, and instead one of connection and empowerment. I have spoken with some elders who say that when we lose connection with the land, the land will die, and so will we. Their words carry even more weight now, as warming weather reshapes the landscape. I feel as though in reconnecting with the mountains I am trying to stop another dispossession, this time from climate change.

My urge to summit and ski the mountains that have formed my identity as a Navajo person has also been motivated by realizing what I call my own "cultural mortality", tied to the existence of these places. Navajo cultural traditions could die along with the alpine landscapes to which they are bound as climate change irreparably alters their composition. The stories that these alpine landscapes hold will no longer have the same meaning.

I started this journey wanting to document photos and stories from the sacred mountains and rivers so that I

It was at that point that I viscerally understood why my culture, like many others, holds mountains and alpine landscapes as sacred.

could impart their teachings for generations to come. But as I visited these places, the path has felt akin to doing the final rounds of visits to my elders, who are sick and soon to walk on into the next world. I needed to begin melding my own story into those held in these landscapes.

A NEW MEANING

As a young person on the Navajo Nation, the stories of the six sacred Navajo mountains did not hold much meaning to me. For many years, I had not realized that these places referenced in ceremonies actually existed. At one point, I even thought they were made up. I vividly remember on my first ski mountaineering adventure on Quandary Peak in Colorado, standing upon a snow-packed ridgeline gazing upon the layers of mountain ranges that rippled westward toward the horizon. My realization of the sacredness of mountains did not fully arrive until I experienced this solitude and stillness. Below my feet on that peak was water that would form the Colorado River in just a few months— a river we see as sacred and which provides our community with life in the desert.

It was at that point that I viscerally understood why my culture, like many others, holds mountains and alpine landscapes as sacred. My skin track became the path of balance and my movement the prayers which I carried. Through ceremony and adventures in these landscapes I understand the power of this form of water, the immense respect and diligence it requires, and the fragility of the climate that fosters it. With some understanding of history, I now know why I once was so disconnected from these mountains.

As the words of our sacred mountains left my lips on the summit of Dook'o'oosłííd, images from that first backpacking ski trip filled my mind—not only with how much had changed within this landscape, but also within me. Until this moment, singing this song, I never responded to the mountain because I didn't know how. The mountain songs afforded me a chance to say thank you. The teachings that they passed to me formed another link in our long-standing connection to this place, reminding me of my role in this continuing cycle of seasons that I now stood within.

LEFT The view from the top offers solitude and stillness.

GETTING TO KNOW SCOOT

📍 LOCATIONS   **ARGENTINA, WEST COAST OF US**

PEOPLE   **EUAN FRASER**

ACTIVITY   **HIKING, SURFING**

ABOVE Euan's 1986 VW campervan was the ticket to some of the best times of his life.

Getting to
know Scoot

EUAN FRASER

"Scoot" was my dad's nickname. I'm not sure why, or where it came from, but I know he had a red, blue, and white woolen hat with Scoot knitted into the front. I know that when he started making climbing and hang gliding harnesses for his friends, Scoot was the name he used for his company. From pictures, stories, and a scattering of memories, I know he loved nature and the outdoors. But I don't really know *him*—because on 2 August 1993, alone in a field, he took his own life.

That day, my mum faced the impossible task of telling three young children that their dad was gone. She told us that he'd died in a hunting accident. Then, she set about the task of being parent enough for both of them —something she managed with room to spare.

I don't know exactly when, but from a young age I became suspicious that my dad didn't die in an accident. I knew the kind of gun he used. I knew he was a careful gun owner. I knew he was alone. Though we talked about dad and had pictures of him around the house, it seemed there was a depth of conversation we all avoided. I thought about him and what happened a lot, but for nearly 20 years I kept it all to myself. I didn't want to upset anyone, and I really didn't want to be right.

LETTING GO OF A SECRET
Years later, as an adult studying in Denmark, away from my family in Scotland, I decided I wanted to know for sure. I thought solving the mystery might help me move

There's few better feelings than drifting off to sleep with salt in my hair, a smile on my face, and the sound of crashing waves in the distance.

THIS PAGE Enjoying the best of times at Short Sand Beach, OR.

on. I ordered a copy of his death certificate and when an official-looking envelope arrived, the words inside didn't surprise me. "Cause of death: contact gunshot wound to the head."

I then went through a pretty tumultuous period—I was angry, sad, lost, and confused. Every time I went home to see mum I'd psych myself up to ask her about what happened, but I just couldn't bring myself to do it. I didn't want her to think she'd done something wrong, or to seem ungrateful for everything she'd done for our family.

Just before my 26th birthday I moved to America and tried to get on with my life. But holding this all inside wasn't working.

In the lonely aftermath of a breakup, I realized that shielding this secret had been part of every relationship I'd ever had. Family, friends, partners… I'd kept them all away from the thing I needed them to understand most. I needed to talk about what happened. And when I called my mum back in Scotland from my new home in Seattle, she told me everything.

Dad suffered terribly with depression. He felt like a failure, like he was constantly letting people down.

Despite having a family he loved and choosing gardening over a career that stressed him out, he couldn't shake his demons. Unfortunately, he believed that all he could do was ride his mood right down to the bottom before coming back up. Sadly, on this occasion he rode it past the point of no return, went out to hunt rabbits, and never came home.

As mum explained this to me, I felt relieved that we were no longer alone with our secrets. I also recognized the feelings she described. I knew the non-specific-but-real feeling of letting people down. Of feeling like a bad person, feeling sad and numbed and scared of the world. When I learned how dad died I got a twisted version of something I'd wanted for a long time: a closer, deeper bond with him.

But I also knew I didn't want to end up like him. I didn't want to be lonely or scared of how I felt. I wanted to have a full and honest relationship with the world and people around me.

Over the next few years I became much more open about what happened. I discovered that sharing my story of losing dad brought people closer rather than pushing them away. We finally talked about it as a family, letting go of a secret that didn't need to be kept.

A DIFFERENT LENS

Not long before the 25th anniversary of that dreadful day, I took a spontaneous trip to Patagonia in Argentina. Thanks to my naivety and poor planning I found myself in El Calafate during shoulder season, in below freezing temperatures, without any of the clothes I should really have brought. Embracing the fact that there were barely any other visitors, and wearing pretty much every layer I had, I set out to explore the Laguna Nimez Nature Reserve.

Hearing the slow crunch of snow beneath my feet, I watched the wind sweep clouds to meet their reflection in the lake in front of me. I felt like the only person on earth. Surrounded by epic nature, I had a sudden and overwhelming realization: *dad would have loved this.* It made me so happy, so grateful to think of him in his element. To imagine him looking round in awe the same way I was now. Maybe he'd know what kind of bird just swooped by.

The next day, following a friend's recommendation, I took a three-hour bus ride to El Chaltén, a small village in Los Glaciares National Park. On my first morning I left the deserted hostel, made a quick stop for breakfast, and walked along the Avenida San Martin to the Laguna de Los Tres trailhead.

It was almost completely dark at the trailhead but light met me at the top of the first ascent, the early rays of sunshine dancing off the frosty grass and bushes. Luckily—dressed as I was in black Levi's, Converse, and two sweatshirts under a thin puffy—the majority of the trail was gentle and as the sun pushed higher into the sky everything warmed up. I stripped off layers, refilled my water bottle in the stream, and was rewarded at every turn with a gorgeous new perspective.

LEFT At Laguna Nimez, Argentina, the vast, epic view changed how Euan related to his father.

From that trip onward, I could see dad through a different lens.

Soon *Los Tres*—the three peaks of Fitz Roy, Poincenot, and Saint-Exupéry—came into view high above me. The ancient jagged aliens beckoned me closer—I'd never seen something unflinchingly still feel so alive. I watched the mountains stretch and morph as clouds flirted round their tops. None of the photographs I took came close to matching what I saw or felt—a huge, blissful solitude. Sitting on a rock eating the two empanadas I'd bought that morning, I couldn't have been more delighted to be alive.

From that trip onward, I could see dad through a different lens. When I looked back at my memories or talked to people who knew him, I saw more of the sensitive, adventurous, creative man I'd only caught glimpses of as a kid. As a teenager, Scoot would hitchhike to the Cairngorms National Park in the north of Scotland just to sleep in the mountains. As he got older he'd make gear and equipment with his own hands if he, or a friend, couldn't find it. He loved to spend time under, or in, the sky: climbing, hang gliding, camping, and skiing. He adored nature with all his being. And I've realized I do too.

Those days in Argentina rekindled my love for getting outside. Since then I've spent more time doing it, and I've gotten better at it. I quit my job at a creative agency and started work at an outdoor company, REI Co-op. I bought a 1986 VW campervan and had some of the best times of my life camping and surfing with friends on the West Coast. Frozen wetsuits; coffee at sunrise; smooth pop-ups and humbling bailouts; sunset sessions turning into moonlit rides on dark, glassy water; a freshly cracked Rainier; lovingly made meals and laughs around the campfire. There's few better feelings than drifting off to sleep with salt in my hair, a smile on my face, and the sound of crashing waves in the distance—ready to wake up and do it all again.

Exploring this shared passion for the outdoors, decades apart, gives me a cherished window into who dad was when he was on good terms with the universe. More importantly, it reminds me to keep finding ways I can experience my own existence in vivid and fulfilling ways.

I might not be able to get to know Alasdair David Watt Fraser, or what it's like to have him as a dad. But I'm sure I get to know Scoot a bit more every time I go outside and lose myself in nature. After decades of wondering why he's gone, I'm beginning to understand why my dad was here—and ready to keep exploring why I am, too.

The *Gift*

FITZ CAHALL

Recognizing the ridiculousness of the current moment, they fell asleep chuckling with each other.

LEFT Becca high up in the Colorado mountains.

"This is colder than Mount Everest," said Becca Skinner's dad. He would know; Becca grew up with stories of her father and grandfather's almost successful summit bid on the world's tallest mountain. When she was in elementary school, her father brought in the crampons he used and gave a presentation on the mountain. Her classmates stared in awe, but to Becca it was just how her family operated. Her parents honeymooned by climbing Ecuador's tallest peak, Chimborazo. Her Uncle Todd, one of the best climbers of his generation, appeared on the cover of *National Geographic*. Becca followed in her family's footsteps, making a career in conservation and outdoor photography.

But, in December of 2014, the predicament they found themselves in appeared to be a step too far for the Skinner family. There's an old truism—be careful what you ask for. Becca was living the inverse—be careful

what you give. Surrounded by her dad, mom, brother, and sister in the confined space of a 150-sq-ft firelook tower, the family seemed one poorly placed comment from outright mutiny.

"No one is having fun. Everyone's cold. Everyone's hungry," says Becca. "When my dad gets angry or really stubborn, he won't make eye contact. He was wearing all his layers. His hood was up. He was looking down at the table. I was like 'This is your birthday cake, Dad. You love cheesecake.' He just said, 'No.'"

SEASON OF LIGHTS

While most of America recovered from Christmas with copious amounts of televised football and endless social media scrolling, Becca had envisioned something more adventurous. A day earlier on Christmas morning, she doled out gifts to her family. Her sister tore off wrapping

THE GIFT

LOCATIONS   **THE ROCKIES, CO**

PEOPLE   **BECCA SKINNER**

ACTIVITY   **HIKING**

ABOVE It seemed like the perfect gift: a night with her family in a remote US Forest Service fire lookout.

Outside, stars would burn bright. In the morning, they'd awake to mountains bathered in perfect alpenglow. But reality had a different plan.

LEFT The Skinner family embrace a walk in snowy conditions.

RIGHT Simple accommodations provides a 360-degree view of the landscape.

paper to find boxed wine. Her mother received Bananagrams, a fun family word game. Her father found a set of rented snowshoes beneath the tree. Her brother opened a headlamp and a card explaining that Becca had reserved one night in a remote fire lookout for the family to enjoy an evening of solitude and winter snow. In Becca's mind, the memory they'd make together would carry through the coming years and that was more precious than anything you could find at a store. The lookout's relative proximity to Denver alleviated detailed planning and if they were just out for one night, how bad could it be?

Becca imagined her family gathered around a warm, wood-fired stove as the mercury dropped in the frigid Colorado winter. Outside, stars would burn bright. In the morning, they'd awake to mountains bathed in perfect alpenglow. But reality had a different plan.

PUBLIC LANDS

America's National Parks grab most of the attention, but the country's National Forest System comprises more than 188 million acres. These landscapes include intact, natural ecosystems, recreational hotspots, and working forests. Founded in 1905, the US Forest Service developed infrastructure to care for the forests, constructing ranger stations and remote fire lookouts atop improbable peaks.

Fueled by the federal government's New Deal—devised to employ Americans during the Great Depression—the Forest Service created a web of what would eventually total 8,000 lookout towers across the country. Over the last 40 years, technology has slowly rendered the use of human lookouts nearly obsolete. An aircraft with a spotter can cover as much ground as 20 lookouts, and is vastly easier to maintain, while live-streaming cameras and satellites have proved to be powerful tools. Hikers themselves, armed with emergency beacons and cell phones, have become part of the warning systems. But culturally, the idea of the lone firelook spending a summer in isolation with a backdrop of mountains and starlit skies resonated with the American psyche.

Today, about 300 fire lookouts remain in operation, though the Forest Service continues to maintain a few hundred more for recreation. Some are first come, first served, and sadly have experienced a glut of overuse. Others can be rented and reserved in advance, ensuring a better experience for hikers, backpackers, and backcountry skiers.

Perched at 11,486ft, the Mestaa'ėhehe Mountain Fire Lookout commands a 360-degree vista of the Colorado Rockies, stretching east toward the Great Plains. It features a small kitchen with a stove, a few cots for sleeping, and a table for eating and playing cards. Everything a visitor hikes in, gets hiked out. To Becca, a night stay sounded like the perfect Christmas for her family, plus an apt early birthday gift for her father. Her enthusiasm was met with blank stares, and more questions than excitement. Still, she persevered and the next day, the Skinner family rummaged through closets for sleeping bags, down jackets, and backpacks.

BOXING DAY

The Skinner family drove an hour west to the small town of Evergreen, CO. It was afternoon by the time they pulled onto the shoulder of the highway and unloaded for their hike up Mestaa'ehehe Mountain. In the blue light of winter dusk, they donned backpacks and snowshoes, enthusiasm momentarily welling up as they marched up the snow-covered road. After 500 yards, the family realized that they would be in the dark,

marching steadily uphill under heavy packs in the cold of a Colorado December for several hours. It was more than even Becca had bargained for.

"No one was having a great time," remembers Becca. "But no one wanted to be the person who said, 'Okay, let's turn around.'"

Their lungs burned in the thin air as snow began to lightly fall before escalating into the beginnings of a blizzard. Becca pushed ahead, hoping to get the fire started, so that her family arrived at a cozy lookout. Panic began to rise when she couldn't get the lock box combination to work. Her sister arrived and, with a fresh wave of calm, they were able to open the lookout. When she swung the door open, she confronted a new reality. On the upper floor, cold poured through the thin panes of the glass windows. In the rock-walled room below, wall-mounted space heaters would prove no match for the cold. Immediately, nervousness and guilt crept in as Becca cranked the heaters to full blast.

A LONG NIGHT
Her family arrived in an explosion of snow and wet gear. They unpacked in silence. Becca offered wine; no takers. A game? Not a chance. They sat through a forgettable meal and by 8 p.m. crawled into sleeping bags for warmth. Becca and her siblings pulled the mattresses from the bunk beds and placed them on the floor so that they could huddle together. Recognizing the ridiculousness of the current moment, they fell asleep chuckling with each other.

In the morning, Becca savored the quiet of the cabin before rising and climbing the stairs to the glass lookout room. The wooden door creaked as she opened it and her parents stirred in their sleeping bags.

"I half-heartedly asked how they slept," Becca says. Her parents, who typically wake well before sunrise, were yet to rise at 8am, having shivered through the night. Neither acknowledged her. "It was not a safe question to ask."

Overnight, the storm had cleared out and sunshine poured in through the windows, bringing with it the slightest hint of warmth. Outside, the wraparound deck immersed them in the Rocky Mountains. Snow glittered on rocky outcroppings. Ridges stretched as far as the eye could see with trees speckled with snow. It was hard to be angry. Becca set to work preparing the breakfast feast she had hiked in. The family sat around the table, steam rising from the food in front of them. Conversation alighted into laughter. Spirits higher, warmth in their bellies, the Skinners packed up. Outside, an untouched layer of snow burned white in the sunshine. With gravity on their side and lighter packs, they began breaking trail downhill.

At the car, Becca's dad let out a soft chuckle. "You know that was fun," he said. "But I hope you don't try and outdo yourself next year."

HAZE OF MEMORY
Years later, Becca's gift has entered into Skinner family lore as the "worst, best vacation they've ever taken" as the family laughs and jokes about it over their Christmas dinners.

"That's not exactly what I was going for with that gift," says Becca. "But in terms of giving an experience where we could share and bond, I think that is what I wanted. To give this gift of adventure, fun, play, and weather. I think walking away with a shared story where all of us were together and something was hard and now we are on the other side of it laughing—that was perfect."

Comfortable moments, after all, don't always make for the best memories.

Adapted from reporting by Ashlee Langholz

LEFT Views are only a small part of a shared experience.

"... walking away with a shared story where all of us were together and something was hard and now we are on the other side of it laughing —that was perfect."

VENTURE OUT

📍	LOCATION	**LONG TRAIL, VT**
	PEOPLE	**PERRY COHEN**
	ACTIVITY	**HIKING**

ABOVE Trail running was where Perry first felt in synch with his body.

Venture *Out*

FITZ CAHALL

RIGHT The Long Trail runs along the Green Mountains in Vermont.

RIGHT The Long Trail runs along the Green Mountains in Vermont.

"It's that look that, if you've ever been a marginalized person, you'll recognize immediately because somebody's sizing you up," says Perry Cohen. "They're trying to figure out what to say and you're trying to figure out, *what's my escape route to get away from this person? Because I don't feel safe.*"

Rooted in our most basic biological functions is the ability to identify a threat. The feeling is unmistakable. Perry was leading a group of a dozen backpackers on the Long Trail, one of America's classic hiking routes and a bucket list trip for seasoned backpackers. Spanning 272 miles, with 70 established backcountry campsites, The Long Trail runs the length of Vermont along the spine of the Green Mountains. The hiking can be rocky, rooty, and muddy, with many remote sections. The effort is rewarded by shelters on the edges of small

ponds and deep vistas of the layered mountains, forests, and small hamlets in the valleys below.

The tired group stopped for the night at one of the trail's open-air wooden shelters. As they greeted the other lone backpacker, Perry sensed something was off. The man asked a series of questions that pulsed with a growing aggression.

Are you some kind of group?

From a college?

Who are you then?

What are you doing here?

ABOVE Instead of working a desk job, Perry started The Venture
Out Project, which leads backpacking and wilderness trips.

At the time, Perry was in his late 30s. In the midst of hormone therapy and a series of surgeries, Perry's body was shifting from female to male, a stage often described as a second puberty. During this period, transgender people may appear younger. The group he was leading was made up of other trans men.

A STEEPER PATH

It's tempting to think of the outdoors as a quasi utopian sphere in which bigotry, hate, and racism magically cease to exist. Big open spaces instill a sense of freedom in us. For the privileged, the price of entry is nothing more than sweat and sore muscles. Ask a member of the LGBTQ+ or BIPOC community and you will get a more nuanced answer. Ignorance and hate don't get shed at the trailhead.

For Perry and his group, the isolation of the outdoors and a lack of cell coverage made the situation feel even more tense. They slowly extricated themselves from the conversation and discussed their options as they filtered water from the nearby creek. Everyone was tired and ready to stop, but everyone felt the *feeling* that they knew all too well in the front country.

As unsettling and undesirable as that moment was, for Perry it was bellwether for the idea he'd made a reality. A group of transgender people all discussed the feelings and emotions that can color their day-to-day existence with one another. It was a powerful moment. The outdoors and backpacking had been the conduit.

★★★

Perry grew up outdoors in the forests of rural New Hampshire. As a social and popular high schooler, he convinced his parents to sign him up for Outward Bound, the outdoor education program where sports like backpacking, sailing, trail running, and climbing called to him. But his first trip in the 1990s wasn't the life-changing experience he'd hoped for. As the lone, self-described "butch lesbian teenager", he didn't click with the other students. Moving outdoors lit a fire inside, but the rest of the experience left him wanting.

"I was so concerned about my safety and not wanting to be outed that I didn't have the mental space or the energy to achieve any of those other goals of developing my leadership abilities or developing my confidence," Perry recalls. "I had used up all my energy on trying to keep myself in the closet."

Perry felt like it was his fault that he couldn't connect with the other kids, so he poured himself into the physical stuff. He tried trail running and, for the first time, felt like he was in sync with his body.

"It just felt free and open. You're paying so much attention to routes and rocks and the beautiful view that you're not really thinking about any of the other problems that may be going on in your life," he says.

MAKING A LEAP

Through the next two decades, Perry felt the happiest when physically active outdoors. He worked for the family grocery business, running an HR department that oversaw thousands of employees. He met his partner and they moved through the world as a lesbian couple. They eventually migrated back to the rolling hills of New England. When they decided they wanted kids, Perry carried the twins.

"And so that was a moment where I started to realize how dissociated I actually felt from my body. All these folks were, like, 'Oh, you look amazing. Isn't this incredible?' And I just thought, 'No. I'm thrilled that we're going to have these babies, but I don't like the constant reminder of womanness in me.'"

Three years later, Perry came out as transgender and, with the support of his family, made the transition from his gender assigned at birth.

"I was still working a corporate job," says Perry. "Everyday I was looking out the window thinking, 'Man, those mountains right outside are so beautiful. I wish I was out there.' I thought, 'If I could transition my gender, I bet I could transition my job.'"

"I thought, 'Wouldn't it be amazing if other trans folk could have the opportunity to get outside like I did?'" he remembers.

CREATING A WAY

Perry looked for queer outdoor organizations where he might lead trips or guide, but found none.

"I got kind of despondent for 24 hours, and then I thought to myself, I led a whole corporate HR department. I understand how to run a business. Maybe I should just start one," says Perry.

The moment marked the inception of the Venture Out Project, a not-for-profit leading backpacking and wilderness trips for the queer and transgender community, and supplying training to traditional outdoor educators for building more inclusive programs. Today, the Venture Out Project spans the country, serving LGBTQ+ individuals as well as their family members. Almost every weekend, there are day trips for both the experienced and those new to the outdoors. The multi-day backpacking program continues to grow and the organization even rethought the traditional running race, launching the All of the Above Trail Fest where competitors aren't segmented into gendered categories.

Perry built the program his community desperately needed, and then watched as outdoor companies offered support and funding. As daily verbal and physical aggression has sadly been on the rise, and anti-trans sentiment has become codified into some states' laws, the importance of safe places becomes clearer and clearer. In the right setting, the natural world can be a powerful avenue for connection in a world where transgender people often feel alienated.

"When you put a bunch of queer people together in nature, conversations just start to happen and people bring up topics that they've wanted to talk about for years, but haven't had the folks to talk about it with," says Perry. "And I think the connections happen instantly. And that's the magic. People feel safe. They feel included and in ways that they've been othered or felt on the outside in so many groups."

NAVIGATING TOGETHER

While The Venture Out Project won't put an end to tense moments like the one on the Long Trail, it helps change the calculus of the experience. Gathered by the stream, Perry's group shared their thoughts and concerns openly, building strength and resolve. They all felt it was best to keep moving and avoid a deeper confrontation. Everyone would sleep better. It was far from ideal, but they could navigate it together. These are the seeds of growth, leadership, and belonging that Perry had missed all those years earlier as a teenager.

"We're trying to do something that's stretching our comfort zone and we get to do it in a community," says Perry. "In the rest of the world, we're just mixed in and we never know for sure that we're in a group of like-minded folks. It's really powerful when you don't have to explain yourself and you can just be."

Adapted from reporting by Kyle Norris

RIGHT Perry trail running on Mount Monadnock, NH.

Bear *Witness*

FITZ CAHALL

The logistics of spending an entire year in the wilderness were daunting, but the concerns that kept them awake were different.

Dave and Amy Freeman joke that their first real date was a 1,100 mile kayak circumnavigation of Lake Superior. It was the summer of 2006. Amy had snuck away from her master's studies to guide sea-kayaking in Grand Marais, MN. Dave was already there, running a not-for-profit out of a small office above the kayak store and occasionally picking up shifts guiding. At season's end, they started their paddling adventure. Their friends took bets on whether they'd return not talking or in it for the long haul.

That 57-day journey proved to be a stepping stone to bigger things. Dave was a digital pioneer who had founded the Wilderness Classroom in 2002. As their relationship deepened Amy dove into the effort. Working with teachers across the country, Dave and Amy crisscrossed North America via kayak, canoe, dog sled, and sailboat, beaming environmental science and biology curriculums from the field into classrooms and, in turn, fielding the youngsters' questions. They embarked on a six-month, 3,000 mile bicycle and canoe journey through the Amazon, creating lessons from tiny villages. They followed that up with an 11,700-mile journey by kayak, canoe, and dog sled across North America. Their efforts earned them recognition as *National Geographic* "Adventurers of the Year".

BEAR WITNESS

LOCATIONS	BOUNDARY WATERS, MN
PEOPLE	DAVE AND AMY FREEMAN
ACTIVITY	CANOEING, WILDERNESS LIVING

ABOVE Amy taking water samples to test the water quality of one of the many lakes in the Boundary Waters.

As the first hints of fall appeared in the trees, Amy and Dave knew their time in the wilderness was drawing to a close. They found themselves more nervous about leaving than they had about entering it.

In between expeditions, Ely, MN (population: 3,233) became the couple's base camp, where they guided dog-sled expeditions and canoe trips. It was as close as they got to having a home. This small town of outfitters, summer cabins, and a handful of restaurants serves as the gateway to America's most visited wilderness—The Boundary Waters Canoe Area Wilderness.

For many in the midwestern states, this 1.1 million acres of forests, lakes, and rivers is their first taste of deep nature as families, scout troops, and summer camps make the pilgrimage to slide canoes into the tannin-stained waters and hear the haunting call of loons echoing across the lakes at dawn. On calm mornings, still water creates perfect reflections of sky and forest. On hot summer days, cold water provides perfect relief. Many children first experience the magic of a fish bringing a line tight or the magnetic warmth of a campfire here. It's how a 12-year-old Amy fell in love with the region. Dave's experience was similar, and both gravitated to summer jobs in the Boundary Waters during college with hundreds of other young seasonal employees, but didn't connect until later. In 2010 on the spring equinox, the pair got married on a frozen lake on the wilderness edge with guests arriving via dogsled, skis, or skates.

HARDWORKING WATERWAYS

People have traversed these waters for eons. Pictographs dot rock outcroppings. The Ojibwe people still gather wild rice on the lakes. At the peak of the North American fur trade in the late 1700 and 1800s, the French Canadian Voyageurs used these waters as natural highways. Today, there are over 1,500 miles of established canoe routes and 2200 campsites. Adjacent to Canada's 1.2-million-acre Quetico Provincial Park, this enormous intact ecosystem and watershed funnels water north toward Hudson Bay. Moose, bear, wolves, and lynx define the landscape and draw in visitors hoping to catch a glimpse by slowing down.

"The water here is really special," says Dave. "I often don't even carry a water bottle, just a little cup so I can just dip it over the side of the canoe. There aren't very many places left in the world where you can do that."

Despite being one of America's earliest designated wilderness areas and its most visited, the Boundary Waters became a focal point for the debate over the value of healthy water and short-term economic gain.

On a busy summer weekend, the town of Ely bustles with visitors and seasonal employees. It belies the fact that the recreation economy hasn't been able to feed everyone. The town's population has fallen as the mining booms of previous decades came and went. Mining, particularly for iron, is a part of Minnesota's hardworking culture and an economic driver; the iron ore, which became the key ingredient in steel, built American cities, bridges, and war ships.

The topic of mining produces a mix of emotions. Nostalgia and pride in some—but for others, new project proposals stirred a deep distrust for the boom-bust economies, industry's promise to clean up after themselves, and mining's human and environmental toll. By no means a new debate, Bob Dylan captured these tensions in the songs he wrote about his home state in the 1960s.

Congress protected the Boundary Waters as wilderness in 1964. In 1978, they went one step further and banned mining in 220,000 acres surrounding the wilderness to provide a buffer. In between, though, the government issued mining leases and kept quietly renewing them. The leases sat dormant, seemingly set to become moot when they expired in 2013, until a multi-international mining company partnered with a local one to see if they could develop the claim with advanced technology and find a windfall on the rising copper price.

The two newly proposed copper mines, run by Twin Metals, were novel to Minnesota. Sulfide-ore mining is a style favored in arid places. When exposed to water and air, the tailings from sulfide ore leach sulfuric acid —essentially battery acid—which kills off the sensitive animals and plants that form the foundation of the food chain. If that acid gets into a water system, it will leach heavy metals out of the surrounding rocks and into the water table, making it unfit for drinking. To place a mine like this on the plateau between two of the continent's largest freshwater basins invited disaster. The issue quickly divided the community, gaining statewide and national attention.

A STEP FORWARD

Getting involved politically didn't come naturally to Dave and Amy, but when they wandered into the newly created Save the Boundary Waters Education Center on Ely's main street in the summer of 2013, in front of them sat a mustard-colored canoe. Adorned with more than 2,000 signatures supporting protections to the watershed, the plan was to load the canoe onto a trailer and deliver it to the Obama administration in Washington DC, along with thousands of more petitions and letters.

"They admired the canoe, but told me that they felt that a canoe should be delivered to President Obama by water and that they wanted to paddle the canoe from Ely to Washington DC," remembers Becky Rom, who spearheaded the campaign. Becky sensed the powerful public relations impact it might have. "That's a long way, but I said, 'Sure.'"

"We were nervous," says Dave. "We don't want to rock the boat. We're quiet people. So we were really concerned that people were going to be yelling at us. It was hard for us to put ourselves out there."

Setting off in August 2014, that 101-day, 2,000-mile journey took them first through the wide open Great Lakes, and then the tight canals and sloughs of the urban corridor. Along the way, they stopped to do presentations and add more signatures to the hull. It was quirky. It was determined. Some might say it was very Minnesotan. Most importantly, it caught people's attention. The head of the US Forest Service met them and whisked them into meetings with various elected officials.

"As much as we hoped we could wave a magic wand and the Boundary Waters would be saved," says Amy, "that experience made it apparent that we would need to keep working on this issue."

Sensing the growing threat to its mining plans, an international mining conglomerate bought Twin Metals and put forth a plan for a $2.8 billion mine with a promise to inject money and jobs into the local community. A touchstone for millions, the Boundary Waters held a place in many people's hearts beyond Ely. Could the Freemans take the Wilderness Classroom model and apply it to activism by bearing witness to this place and broadcasting that experience to the greater world?

A YEAR IN THE WILDERNESS

On September 23, 2015, Amy and Dave slid their canoe into Birch Lake. Surrounded by a flotilla of friends ushering them into the next year, they paddled toward the South Kawishiwi River. The flotilla stopped. The Freemans kept paddling. Deviously simple and humbly bold, Amy and Dave planned to live for a year inside the Wilderness area. Through the shortening days and explosion of fall leaves turning brilliant yellow, they would paddle. When the cold came and before the lakes iced over, they made camp until winter snow blanketed the forest and lakes. Then they'd use skis and sled dogs to travel to new lakes. In spring, cracks sliced across the lake ice, so the duo would have to push the canoe like a toboggan, leaping in as it entered the water.

BELOW Dave and Matt prepare to hit the water.

Until the ice broke up and travel by canoe became easier, they treaded lightly. With the growing warmth, they'd watch as the forest and animals flourished in the Minnesota summer.

The logistics of spending an entire year in the wilderness were daunting, but the concerns that kept them awake were different.

"It wasn't bugs or cold or not showering for a year," says Amy. "It was that people would forget about us. That we wouldn't be effective. We quickly learned that that was not something we had to be scared about because people wanted to help out in any way they could."

Instead, their actions piqued interest. Suddenly, campaign managers at Save the Boundary Waters were fielding requests to visit. Some days there would be as many as three groups—concerned citizens, journalists, and elected officials—who paddled or dog-sledded into the wilderness to chat with the Freemans or provide resupplies. The outfitters and guides in Ely helped shuttle guests back and forth. The legend began to grow. Canoeists spontaneously stopped to chat and took photos. They'd carry the Freemans' story and message back to family and social media channels. Online, people followed, and the campaign would go on to represent a coalition of 18 million people via an array of recreation, tribal, veteran, fishing, and conservation organizations.

The year sped by in a series of moments the Freemans carried with them. The gray blur of a wolf trotting silently across the opposite shore. Chopping a hole in

THIS PAGE Snow fun on a frozen lake.

ice provided access for the monthly bathing dip and the burn of cold water. Lakes crossed in blizzard conditions and disorienting whiteouts. Wandering into what remained of the last ancient old growth stands in the Midwest. The first warm days of spring and the relief they brought after the long winter. The rustle of snow-white trumpeter swans' wings as they landed in fields of wild rice. The long days of summer light.

As the first hints of fall appeared in the trees, Amy and Dave knew their time in the wilderness was drawing to a close. They found themselves more nervous about leaving than they had about entering it. They were needed back in the "real" world; the struggle for the Boundary Waters was in full swing as President Obama entered the final months of his presidency. On September 23, 2016, they packed up their camp for the final time. Friends appeared. On the final portage, which typically requires multiple trips back and forth to carry the boat and gear between two lakes, well-wishers appeared to congratulate and thank them by carrying their packs along the trail. As they crossed beneath the highway bridge, the television cameras appeared. Seventy canoes converged around the Freemans, leading them into shore, as they fought back tears. In the flotilla, they lingered, delaying their return to land.

★★★

Three days later, they flew east in the recycled air of a plane. Hours later, they'd be in front of the bright television lights of the *Today* show and in the halls of Congress, making their case for the Boundary Waters. In Minnesota, they had reached folk hero status. Prompted to speak up for their home, they'd acted in their own quiet, determined way. Comments poured in to elected officials. Ely awaited the decision.

That December, the phone rang. On the other end of the line, Becky relayed the news. The Forest Service and Bureau of Land Management had just denied the Twin Metals leases and announced a two-year moratorium on any mining-related activity on federal land inside the watershed. The Freemans smiled and cried simultaneously. It wouldn't mean an end to threats against the Boundary Waters, but the efforts had worked this time.

"There's no one way to act," says Dave. "The key is to figure out what you're passionate about and what you're good at, and leverage those skills."

Amy adds, "It seems kind of obscure—how can a couple of wilderness guides and educators do something to effect change? I think that no matter what your skills are, you can figure out a way to apply them and protect whatever place it is that you care about."

Postscript: In the years that followed, the Freemans and Save the Boundary Waters saw the Trump administration reverse course on the mining decision. Through a combination of grassroots organizing, outreach, and legal action, the mining efforts were stymied. In 2023, almost 10 years after the Freemans' original paddle to DC, the Biden administration established a 20-year moratorium on mining.

Contains reporting from Jen Altschul

PREVIOUS SPREAD
The breathtaking purity of the Boundary Waters would be ruined forever if mining was allowed.

BELOW Dog sleds helped the pair to travel during winter.

Sleeping Bag
Metamorphosis

ANYA MILLER BERG

I grew up in eastern Canada in a family that wasn't really that outdoorsy. My sisters, my brother, and I were active, but only in traditional sports—gymnastics, swimming, soccer, track. My family had two musty things that we called sleeping bags; ridiculously heavy brown canvas, itchy wool, flannel, metal zipper, both as wide as a twin bed and about as unwieldy to carry.

These sleeping bags had to be some relic of a trip where either a car or a large animal helped bring them to a resting point. I hated getting one out for any reason because I couldn't put it away by myself. It was a two-kid job to wrestle that thing back into a giant, submissive roll.

Somewhere along my traditional sporting path, I began to change. I'm fairly sure it started in gymnastics class, but I really started to pay attention to my new calling while out running on a dirt double-track I had ambitiously dubbed a trail in college. I became obsessed with the idea of being outside, getting dirty, moving through the landscape, and then stopping in the middle of it. I wanted to get out and to be out. I realized that when you can sleep anywhere, you can go anywhere.

A HOME AWAY FROM HOME

I remember going to buy it. I was a little worried about the money, but I knew that anything I actually wanted to do in life, literally anything, depended on a proper sleeping bag. After a summer of bussing tables and lifeguarding, I'd saved up enough and I was finally going to get a sleeping bag. My first sleeping bag. My ticket to anywhere I wanted to be.

At the MEC store, I laid out a bag on the thinly carpeted floor and zipped myself in. I drew the hood tight and closed my eyes, imagining opening them and finding myself in Bishop, Waco, Argentina, France, a friend's couch, the back of a Subaru, in the snow, on the dirt. Women's medium, winter rating, right-hand zip. Done.

SLEEPING BAG METAMORPHOSIS

LOCATIONS	**USA, AUSTRALIA, CHILE, FRANCE**
PEOPLE	**ANYA MILLER BERG**
ACTIVITY	**CLIMBING**

LEFT Warming up on the Buttermilks' tacky granite in spring.

It took me somewhere I wasn't. It took me away from being sick. It reminded me that I was a vigorous person, a healthy person, a person who had slept out under the stars, in the rain, and under a tailgate or a boulder.

ABOVE The rock face at Mount Arapiles.

My sleeping bag became more of a personal place than I ever imagined. My unwashed, chalky, dirty, cold, exhausted self could climb in and always feel totally at home. Lend that space out? Uhmm, I've got an extra blanket you can use. My pillow? Sure. But my bag? No. Sorry, not sorry. I think I'm going to be using it.

DAY IN, DAY OUT
And I used it.

A month in the San Juans with the Colorado Outward Bound School, surfing down granite scree fields by day, sleeping under the stars by night. Bright orange petals of Indian paintbrush. Alpine bouldering. Sudden downpours. Wet down. I loved falling asleep like this.

Study abroad to Australia where online courses allowed me to ditch Sydney and focus on my preferred areas of study. Tiger-striped rock of the Grampians, cliffs seemingly perched on the edge of wide valleys in the Blue Mountains, the contrasting greens and oranges of Mount Arapiles. I peeked out of my cocoon, realizing I was becoming the person I always wanted to be. I knew because the little joeys in our camp told me so. I loved waking up like this.

A hostel in Via Nevado, Chile, with icy showers in wintry August. Tongue out to the left, knob turn to the right, light the pilot. Hop in the shower. Nope. Still cold. Quick soap up. Forget the shampoo, rinse, rinse, rinse, hustle down the hall, jump in and zip up. Vigorous sit-ups in my bag to jumpstart warmth. I loved falling asleep like this.

Fontainebleau on a stony floor made marginally better by the buffer of my bouldering pad. Morning sensations of coffee wafting in. Fingertips sanded, raw, weeping. I wake up and stuff my sleeping bag away to tidy the small, quaint space. First hand pain of the day, forcing my sleeping bag into its ridiculously small sack. I loved waking up like this.

A bright dark night in my frosted Subaru. Buttermilks, USA. I should have camped in the Tablelands. Maybe I'll start the car for a few minutes just to warm up. My eyes flutter open. Wait. Holy shit. What is that? Get it off me. A lighted bug is right next to my face. Oh, wait.

Okay. Okay. It's a glow in the dark zipper pull. Classic. Gear designers are smart. I loved falling asleep like this.

My sleeping bag was my place to contemplate the things I did that day. To replay a sweet pattern, a hilarious conversation with friends, a rad view. It's also my place to dream, my place to conceive of goals I wanted to tackle next, and my place to get up the gumption to really plan them out. I'd close my eyes, make a decision, and wake up in the morning a new me, convinced that I was totally capable and that anything was possible.

A PLACE OF COMFORT

September 2, 2011. The automated hospital doors slid open, releasing me into the warm air and golden light of late summer in Seattle. A series of tests had just shown that I had cancer. Two months and four chemo treatments deep, I crawled into my sleeping bag. Not hungry is an understatement, but my body was buzzing with energy. Not the good kind of energy that makes a person jump up and go run around in the mountains. The kind that perpetually alerts all of your nerves to the fact that there is something very wrong. The kind that fatigues you past the point of being able to sleep. I tried to read, but that didn't really take. Even holding a book up was hard.

Tired of being in bed, being in one place, I would pad out to the couch with my sleeping bag in tow. Netflix as my ally, I holed up in my down-filled sanctuary for hours upon hours of *Mad Men*, *Law & Order*, and *The Wire*. Through those few months that seemed to last years, my sleeping bag also proved to be a place for me to think about the things that I didn't get to do on any given day. Like Linus's security blanket, that thing just made me feel better. It took me somewhere I wasn't. It took me away from being sick. It reminded me that I was a vigorous person, a healthy person, a person who had slept out under the stars, in the rain, and under a tailgate or a boulder. And it gave me hope that I would be that type of person again.

★★★

Luckily, I am me again. I run, climb, ride, scramble, sleep, repeat. That day I bought my first sleeping bag, my perspective of where I could go and what I could do transformed. My sleeping bag is a place and a mindset that has allowed me to weather a storm. When you can sleep anywhere, you can go anywhere. And when you can go anywhere, you can do anything.

LEFT Amy and her cocoon which she refuses to share.

Chapter Four
Thru-Life

Green *Light*

FITZ CAHALL

In November 2015, Becca gave birth to our second son, Wiley. Interrupted sleep and diapers became routine. Often, after working long days and caring for the boys, when the kids were down and the dishes done, Becca and I would use the hours every parent normally cherishes to relax and reset to power out some solution to an issue at work. Pre-kids, I'd made pre-dawn ski laps a routine, but that winter I didn't have the energy.

One clear winter afternoon on my way to pick up my son Tep, I sat motionless in traffic on I-5. A surge in tech jobs had recently seen Seattle join the likes of New York City and Los Angeles in having some of the worst traffic in the nation. But this bumper-to-bumper sea of brake lights came with a particularly torturous perk—a million-dollar view. Looking out over a sailboat-dotted Lake Union toward the snow-capped Olympic Mountains, my gaze fell to the centerpiece of the range —the Brothers. As the backdrop of the city skyline, the twin summits anchored countless postcards and Hollywood movie scenes. I imagined the deep settling cold and a resonant quiet. Then I almost rear ended the car in front of me. I felt stuck.

SET YOUR SIGHTS
At the age of 19, I came to Seattle because it had two things in abundance—mountains and music. The place felt like an opportunity; a person could never

LEFT A short lunch break overlooking a few of the 266 glaciers and permanent snowfields in Olympic National Park.

At the age of 19, I came to Seattle because it had two things in abundance—mountains and music.

GREEN LIGHT

📍 LOCATIONS	**OLYMPIC NATIONAL PARK, WA**
PEOPLE	**FITZ CAHALL**
ACTIVITY	**SKIING, SNOWBOARDING**

ABOVE A quick scramble between snow fields is adventure skiing at its best.

I decided to put the Brothers at the top of the list. I wasn't going to stare longingly at that peak from traffic any longer.

realistically have an excuse to be bored. That first winter, I slept underneath a parked car, waiting in line for the REI garage sale while the rain fell and hundreds of people milled around for a crack at deeply discounted outdoor gear in the retailer's underground parking lot. I bought a pair of climbing boots, crampons, and an old rental ice axe. I never looked back.

While young climbers talked incessantly about Washington's highest peak, the 14,411ft Mount Rainier that dominates the view to the southeast from Seattle— I bought a guide to the Olympics instead. "One day soon," I thought, "I'm going to go climb the Brothers." That was almost 20 years ago. Somehow the Brothers fell down the list.

In the intervening years, Becca and I cultivated a wonderful garden of a life, working hard to build a community and creative business while taking time to explore the deserts and mountains of the American West in long days that often began and ended in the dark. Now with a family, we centered our free time around getting our family outdoors on child-sized adventures where the pace slowed and the scale tightened, revealing a different sort of magic. But the

garden required near constant care, and we knew that the days dedicated to fulfilling those hard-to-achieve, personal outdoor goals—the ones some might deem selfish, too time-intensive, risky, certainly diaper-free —were important too.

We developed a plan to help each other create four days a year reserved for the objectives that would push us; leaving us exhausted and a little late for curfew. The other parent would hold down the house.

I flipped through the guidebook and put the Brothers at the top of the list. I wasn't going to stare, longingly, at those peaks from traffic any longer.

A GUARDED MOUNTAIN
Ninety-five percent of Olympic National Park is designated wilderness—raw and vibrant with unruly, unkempt trails that vegetation would erase in a few years if it weren't for the efforts of trail crews. Long approaches at low elevations to steep rugged climbs on crumbling rock and variable snow define the climbing. As my plan formed, I was surprised to learn that no one in my network of ski partners had skied the Brothers or for that matter knew someone who had.

I began to understand why. The mountain is guarded by a 5½-mile approach before any real elevation is gained. It's not quite a day trip, so it requires carrying a heavier pack with overnight gear. Avalanche stability needs to be spot on—slivers of snow reaching a steepness of 55 degrees cut through the rock walls of the eastern flanks. Preferably, an attempt needs a low snowline of around 3,000ft—but not too low or the long, flat approach through dense forest becomes a nightmare. The window for success is small.

All of us are drawn to the improbable, but with the reality of the day to day, the small weekend window, and the traffic guarding an easy exit from the city, we often settle for the likely, where straightforward approaches weigh the odds towards success.

In a sea of red lights, you need a green.

THE WINDOW OPENS
In late March, a window appeared—but between family commitments and partner availability it soon closed. Another opened in April. I started making frantic calls for partners, but the temperature spiked into the low 80s and the mountains became a tangle of avalanche debris. We called it off. Our family traveled to Colorado for two weeks. By the time we returned, the mountains had been doused by rain and hot weather. The spring thaw was six weeks ahead of schedule. It looked like I'd spend another year in traffic.

But my luck changed. A window appeared—a Thursday afternoon and Friday just before Mother's Day weekend, free of work meetings and deadlines.

I called a friend who had been ski guiding for the previous two weeks. Things had melted out fast, he reported. Becca dug up a terse trip report from the northern end of the Olympics, laced with ominous phrases like "rotten snow", "low coverage", and the ever-damning "ski season is over". It seemed like while weather and work offered a green light, the Olympics had other ideas.

And yet, stuck on I-5, in a dense cluster of Seattle traffic, I peered west. There they loomed: lofty, intimidating, and *maybe* just snow-covered enough. I'd certainly never be able to ski them from the safety of Seattle. I decided to go; failure was a definite option.

VALLEY OF THE SILENT MEN
I left work early on Thursday, repacking my bag on the ferry as it traversed the Puget Sound toward the Olympic Peninsula. I'd need to be as light as possible to pull this off in 24 hours. No tent. No stove. No coffee.

I started the hike in as the light faded. A few hours later, when I hit a tangle of fallen trees, I decided to sleep underneath the Valley of the Silent Men's giant cedars. Here, Lena Creek goes underground; the murmur of water, deep below the earth, carried me to sleep.

At daybreak I set out, swiftly turning off the established trail. Five miles in, I reached the beginning of the climb and steady succinct snow. Kick step, kick step, plant the ice axe. Breathe. Repeat. I started counting my steps, trying to take 100 at a time. The route revealed itself slowly, curving between rock gullies. A long hour of maximum exertion brought me almost to the top. I dropped my snowboard and scrambled between exposed ribs of rock to small patches of snow for the final 50ft. A mountain goat reluctantly gave up its throne atop the summit and skittered over to another peak, while I slumped into a pile of gear, exhausted.

It was a perfect day in the Olympics, not a cloud in sight and no wind. To the west, the heart of the park extended outward in a maze of deep valleys, glaciers, and rocky peaks—a glimpse into another lifetime of exploration. I looked at a series of gentle ridges and imagined a day when the kids were older, and Becca and I might be regular adventure partners again. I imagined Tep and Wiley walking along the rolling ridge of the Olympic National Park's Deer Park. It would make a perfect backpacking route. I felt happy.

THE SPACE BETWEEN
I turned back east, toward home. Mount Rainier cast a deep shadow. To the north, Mount Baker's glaciers burned white in the morning light. Between the peaks, sunlight poured through the canyons created by Seattle's skyscrapers. I followed the city's skyline north past the Space Needle to the hill where we lived. I imagined Tep at school, looking forward to a weekend of Saturday cartoons, wrestling with dad, and riding his bike. Wiley would likely be dozing in a stroller. If the rest of the day went well, I'd be home in time to put them to bed. That made me happy too.

To the west, was an entire range of ideas, dreams, and potential memory. To the east, all the wonderment, joy, and belonging I'd worked to build. I stood perched between them. On one hand, this perspective could be considered hard-earned—18 miles on foot, 7,000ft of elevation gain, stumbling through slide alder—but that morning it struck me how close those two places really are: physically, spiritually, emotionally. It's a matter of making the space to weave them together.

Ten minutes later, I scrambled down to my snowboard. I clipped in and edged the board out, studying the terrain for hazards and safe spots. I visualized my first turns, where a fall would be bad. As always, I took three deep breaths and began arcing turns toward home. The light was as green as it was ever going to get.

FLYING DEEP

📍 LOCATION	**CANADIAN ROCKIES**
PEOPLE	**WILL GADD AND GAVIN McCLURG**
ACTIVITY	**PARAGLIDING**

ABOVE Soaring like condors above The Rockies.

Flying *Deep*

FITZ CAHALL

"I felt like I was the luckiest human on the planet," says Will Gadd. "Just a magic moment. It's logged into the memory banks and it's a good one."

Will and his co-conspirator Gavin McClurg were spiraling upward, riding thermals up the flanks of the Canadian Rockies' highest peak, Mount Robson. Anchoring the northern end of this world-class mountain range of glaciers, jagged rock ridges, and deep wild valleys, Robson defines the word iconic. "God made mountains, but good God! Who made Robson," remarked the famed Austrian guide and climber Conrad Kain, who made the first ascent of Robson in 1912. Despite the long climbing history, reaching the summit still remains difficult—only about 10 percent of would-be climbers succeed—in part because of the weather.

Through its sheer size, the mountain typically generates its own meteorological systems, hiding itself in clouds, but today the clouds pulled back, making a flight possible. From a distance, their paragliders looked like two condors soaring upward in unison. Over the roar of the wind, Gavin could hear Will laughing maniacally with enthusiasm. Will's idea of what could be done with a paraglider had just expanded.

Will defines the term legend in the mountain communities, performing at the very highest levels in climbing, kayaking, and paragliding. He helped trailblaze the professionalization of mountain sports, laying the groundwork for a generation of adventurers who have made a living practicing their craft. He's climbed a frozen Niagara Falls and owned the world record for longest

ABOVE Will and Gavin's flights took them into deep, unvisited regions.

distance paragliding. Evaluation and mitigation of risk are constant obsessions for Will who is one of the most thoughtful people on the planet on the topic.

That flight over Robson marked the start of an 500-mile paragliding journey down the spine of the Canadian Rockies, another first in Will's long resume.

From the French for "fly camp", the pursuit of Vol Biv is the fringe of the fringe in paragliding terms. A pilot packs what they need to spend the night out. When the wind favors flying, pilots take to the sky, pushing their progress forward. When evening comes or the wind becomes unsuitable, they must find a place to land and set up camp.

In Europe, pilots had set up the earliest races which saw competitors fly from the height of the Alps to the Mediterranean coast, but when Will competed he found himself hiking all his gear forward when conditions weren't right for flying. It seemed more like backpacking than paragliding. It gave him the idea—a journey

where forward progress could only be made via flight. A pilot would need to be patient and move when natural forces allowed.

Will and Gavin charted an invisible line above the Canadian Rockies' spine—they would do their best to fly the entire route. No walking when conditions wouldn't allow flying. For the duo, it was the perfect test of skill, experience, risk management, and commitment. For the world of paragliding, the flight could prove to be a leap forward.

MAPPING THE LINE
Air moves like water in an invisible river. There is a general direction, but also thousands of eddies and chaotic rapids. Great pilots utilize a deep understanding of mountain environments. Without a motor, they must find a thermal—air rushing upward, often in a column —to gain elevation. They might find it above a sunny mountain slope or at the edge of a clear-cut. They look for birds and pay attention to the smell of the wind to understand the direction of the air.

The duo mapped a line: McBride, British Columbia, south to the US border. While Will owned the world record for the longest paragliding flight—263 miles in a single day, achieved in the flatlands of Texas in ideal flying conditions—the terrain and weather they would encounter along the Rockies meant that the journey would likely take weeks. A successful flight might be 20 miles. Flying over some of the most remote and rugged sections of the Canadian Rockies, their thesis for the trip guided them: let the paraglider take you places, versus beelining for the end.

"We had our landscape and we had our style and it was like, 'Alright, let's put that in a blender and see what that tastes like,'" says Will. "Most of my trips it's like, 'Man, wouldn't it be cool to do A, B, and C?' And then we try and go do it with very little actual research. You have a dream and then you go out and try and make it happen."

UPS AND DOWNS
As the days unfolded, Will and Gavin used the wide open alpine terrain to the best of their advantage. The range's upper regions are well above the treeline and can offer wide open slopes and saddles to land in. In the mornings, they might hike a short distance to find a suitable launch point. There, they'd let a growing morning breeze fill the wing and then run full speed downhill until their feet left the ground. Along the way, they landed on the shoulder of Mount Terry Fox—a remote mountain named for the Canadian folk hero and cancer research activist who ran 3,339 miles across Canada after losing his leg to the disease. They explored caves on the side of limestone outcroppings. While the Canadian Rockies offer world-class hiking and trails weave between turquoise glacier lakes that sit in the shadows of glaciers, Will and Gavin saw seldom-visited areas, some inaccessible by foot. They visited alpine regions typically left to the domain of ravens, bighorn sheep, and grizzlies, but the cost of a mistake was also clear.

Landing in the wrong place or suffering an equipment malfunction could easily result in an epic, multi-day walk for survival that would include fording rivers and miles of punishing bushwhacking. This is what paragliders refer to as "flying deep"—the margin for error goes down, the price of a mistake compounds.

"In paragliding, there are some pretty simple rules," explains Gavin. "Don't fly in heavy wind. Don't fly in the lee. Don't fly above places you can't land. We knew we were going to have to break most of those rules on this expedition."

As prevailing winds approach a mountain slope, they rise in predictable manners as the landscape pushes wind up. As that air moves to the backside of a mountain or the lee side, air becomes violently unpredictable. Downdrafts collapse wings, leaving pilots racing to maneuver. It's easy to lose elevation rapidly, but if Gavin and Will wanted to make progress south, they would occasionally need to chance it in the unpredictable lee side of mountains.

As they moved steadily south over three weeks, the weather grew more difficult. In alpine environments, clouds build in the warmth of the day, threatening thunderstorms. Higher winds create turbulence. The updrafts and terrain become more unpredictable. If there are no thermals, you have to land. If there's nowhere to land safely, you crash-land into a tree, boulder field, or steep slope.

"It's kind of like swimming a rapid if you come out of your kayak," explains Will. "Sometimes it's okay. Sometimes it kicks the shit out of you. Sometimes you die. The line is really fine."

Further south, above the 134-mile long Kinbasket Lake, they'd flown roughly 12 miles and were doing their best to eke out more distance in deteriorating conditions. Will gained elevation and snuck over a small ridge, but when Gavin tried, the thermal dissipated. He radioed to Will, but the ridge blocked radio contact. On his own, Gavin hunted for lift as he slowly sank toward rocky terrain. Desperate, Gavin searched for a spot to land with the least amount of rocks where it would be easy to break an ankle. He swung and then it went wrong. He sat in a heap, his first career crash landing, but came out with only minor cuts and bruises. Able to walk, he hiked upward until he was able to make contact with Will and meet up. High up on an alpine ridge with the British Columbia wilds spread in front of them, they made camp for an evening. The stakes were clear, but the reward of charting an invisible path through one of North America's great natural landscapes was abundantly clear too.

A NAGGING UNEASE
The next 12 miles of flying required good weather and the duo's combined decades of experience. Kinbasket Lake guarded their exit. The steep slopes fell straight into the lake, leaving no room for beaches. Slide alder overgrew the old logging roads that crisscrossed the landscape. An emergency alighting would likely result in a water landing or getting hung up in a tree.

"If that happened, we would have had to build a raft and paddle across 30km of lake to get out," says Will, with a hint of mischief.

They waited out one day of bad weather. Then a second. They started rationing food. A third day of bad weather. Finally, conditions allowed them to launch on the fourth.

"We ended up flying 110km that day," Gavin remembers. "It was almost like being taken out of reality for a while. It was like we'd taken some sort of drug that was this combination of adrenaline, fear, and low blood sugar."

As they moved closer to the US border, the weather continued to slow their progress. Will had a nagging sense that they were drifting into uncomfortable terrain.

"No matter what I'm doing, I envision the worst possible scenario and how to deal with it," he reflects. "I visualize and visualize until I'm good with the situation. I don't do it if I can't see it clearly in my head. With so many days of pushing in hard and big conditions, I started to feel like I was getting on the wrong side of the numbers. You can only push so hard before you make a bad decision. On the flipside we had some moments, many moments of sheer magic, like flying a paraglider over the summit of Mount Robson."

After 35 days, Gavin and Will flew the remaining 19 miles to the US Border over a remote valley, 16 miles from the nearest road—something Will might have balked at earlier in the trip. They circled above the border—a clear cut line in the forest—before turning back north. "Gavin and I both would have liked to just have kept going, but I think that would have caused an international incident," says Will. After landing on the edge of a small river on a crisp October day, the pair hugged. They had expanded the definition of "deep" not just for themselves, but for the paragliding community.

LEFT Judging a landing wrong could leave you dangling from a tree.

Mr *Hodges*

FITZ CAHALL

Ed Hodges' zeal for teaching manifested itself in his lessons. If you walked the hallways of Hoover Junior High in San Jose, CL, you might stumble upon a group of biology students with their thumbs taped to their palms. Mr. Hodges sensed that 48 hours without a thumb might instill an appreciation for the role opposable digits played in human evolution.

In a lesson on mechanical advantage, Mr Hodges rigged a pulley system on the tree outside the classroom to prove that one student could overpower 10 in a tug of war, with the right physics. To hammer home a unit on surface area and dispersal of energy, a student lay down with a large flat rock on their chest, while another walloped the rock with a sledgehammer. His teaching style could simultaneously be described as gonzo and practical, but his passion was never in question. He made the subject matter live and breath, and his students loved him for it.

LEFT Mr Hodges gets the maps out.

For the junior high bike club, the transcontinental route they plotted was akin to a high school science club proposing to enter low-earth orbit

MR HODGES

📍 LOCATIONS   **PRINCE RUPERT, BC, TO SAN JOSE, CA**

PEOPLE   **MEGAN HAYES AND THE HOOVER-LINCOLN BIKE CLUB**

ACTIVITY   **BICYCLING**

ABOVE Twenty-two junior high students ride their steel-framed bikes from Canada to San Jose.

A DIFFERENT ERA

Times were different in the 1970s. The country was less
litigiously inclined. In suburban basements, kids played
Pong on Atari game consoles and Black Sabbath played
on the record players of older siblings. Kids rode bikes
through the streets on summer nights and helicopters
were an aircraft, not a form of parenting. Outdoor
sports inhabited a fringe space in America. With the rise
of suburbia and car-commutes to urban centers, the
bicycle's popularity as a mode of transportation had
evaporated since its peak in the early 1900s. In 1884,
Tom Stevens became the first person to ride across the
US, but the concept of long-distance road biking
wouldn't really re-enter America's cultural awareness
until Greg LeMond won the Tour de France three times
in dramatic fashion in the late 1980s and early '90s.

In his love for bikes, Mr Hodges was a forerunner. Rain
or shine, he pedaled a Schwinn Continental, nicknamed
the "Tank" for its heft, to school every morning. For
Megan Hayes and her girlfriends, Mr Hodges held a
certain mystique. They too rode their bikes to school.
In 1971, Megan's group of friends asked Mr Hodges
to sponsor a school cycle group, founding the Hoover
Bike Club.

They started with "short" rides around San Jose and
California's central coast. They pedaled 3,000ft up
Saratoga Gap. Mount Madonna checked in at 40 miles
with 1,800ft of gain. With lighter aluminum frames just
starting to go into production and the feather-weight
carbon frames of today decades out, the kids rode heavy
steel bikes. They loved it, though, and it wasn't long
before the club embarked on weekend-long rides to
Yosemite and through Death Valley. On the roadside, a
group of teenagers, not yet old enough to drive, must
have stood out. Parents had little idea of what their kids
were up to.

"You were unplugged. You were unconnected,"
remembers Megan. "There's a certain liberation
to it. We had that at a pretty young age. It was just
a big adventure the whole time."

The club grew in size. Megan's founding group of
friends moved on to high school, but they incorporated
as the Hoover-Lincoln Bike Club so that they could still
participate in the weekend rides. By 1975, Mr Hodges
had a group of 40 students pedaling along California's
back roads and highways. The club mirrored the diverse
backgrounds and economic circumstances of the San

Jose public school system. No matter the circumstances, the kids dug up cut-off jean shorts, sneakers, and old steel-frame bikes. And each year, they came back asking for more audacious and difficult routes.

"So we started looking at maps," remembers Mr Hodges. "I said, 'Well, what about Alaska?' Kind of outrageous, right? What parent is going to let their kid go with their teacher during the summer for 40 days to Alaska?"

LOOKS GOOD ON PAPER

Twenty-two enthusiastic students pored over maps, planning a 2,500-mile itinerary that started at the Alaskan border, through British Columbia, then down through Washington, Oregon, and Northern California before returning home. The kids needed to average 65 miles a day. For the junior high bike club, the transcontinental route they plotted was akin to a high school science club proposing to enter low-earth orbit. Mr Hodges and his wife, Ramona, would chaperone and provide vehicle support to carry all the camping gear and food. He helped find the necessary equipment and conjured up flexible leather bike helmets for the appearance of safety, but the kids deemed them too nerdy to wear. He required a basic physical fitness

cutoff. Anyone attempting the ride, needed to complete a day-long, 100 mile ride.

On June 21, 1975, 22 kids boarded a train to Washington state, while Mr Hodges and Ramona drove north. From northern WA, they took a ferry to Vancouver Island, mounting the bikes there and pedaling up the rainy coast, hopping another ferry to Prince Rupert, BC, then began their two-wheeled journey home. In interior BC, thick clouds of mosquitoes plagued them, but their bodies adjusted to day-in, day-out riding as they traveled farther than they'd ever been from home. During the long days of pedaling, confidence and enthusiasm began to flourish among the teens. There'd be long stretches where Mr Hodges trusted them to make good decisions while he followed in the van or cycled alongside the slower riders.

GAINING GROUND

Mr Hodges orchestrated the days, dividing the students into cook, clean-up, and camp teams. He'd meticulously planned each meal so that, as the strain of long days' pedaling began to alter the kids' metabolisms, he'd keep up with their calorific needs. From Prince George, the kids followed the Fraser River south toward the US border. Behind the van's steering wheel, Mr Hodges

OPPOSITE PAGE The group poses at the top of Mount Lassen—denim cut-offs were the order of the day.

RIGHT Megan Hayes who initiated the bike club, with her friend Cathy.

LEFT Greg Holmes as a biking superhero.

RIGHT Students carried their missing friends' bikes to the top of Mount Lassen.

watched in horror as lightning struck the road near a group of students during a summer downpour. Unhurt, the kids remember the electricity spider webbing outward on the wet pavement in white heat. To avenge an earlier prank where the kids had faked a horrific bike crash complete with ketchup for blood, Mr Hodges talked a US Customs border guard into pretending to detain the students complete with pat downs at the crossing north of Bellingham, WA. Mr Hodges smiled and laughed as he snapped photos of the bewildered students.

They continued on, south to Seattle before pedaling up into the Cascades and the winding, tree-lined mountain roads around the hulking Mount Rainier. For more than a month, the students worked as a unit under Mr Hodges' guidance, to pull off an improbable trip. Looking back, the students—now grown and many with children of their own—describe it as a moment of powerful bonding, where doors opened to the power of their own potential.

When two students crashed south of Rainier, breaking bones and requiring a hospital visit, the group wrestled with the fact that they'd need to continue without them.

"I was devastated," said Linda Ferensten, who remembers Mr Hodges calling her father and offering to let her ride along in the van. "They chose to fly me home. I had a lot of anger toward my dad. As a parent, now I see, but I was so upset."

The other student chose to return home in solidarity and the group continued south, crossing the Columbia River into the rolling hills of central Oregon, the Cascade volcanoes anchoring the western skyline. After the accident, the teens diligently wore their helmets. In southern Oregon, a stomach bug nearly derailed their progress. On July 21, they crossed into California, regrouping in the shadow of Mount Shasta before pressing onto Lassen National Park, where they paused to climb the 10,457-ft tall Mount Lassen. The kids carried the fallen riders' bikes up the trail summit, to commemorate their fallen friends. In Lake Tahoe, they stopped at one student's family cabin and gorged on the all-you-can-eat buffets at the Nevada casinos.

After six weeks, pedaling up the 8,000-ft passes of the Sierra south of Tahoe felt almost effortless. They streaked down from the Sierra Crest toward the patchwork and green-brown fields of the Central Valley.

THE ROAD HOME

"As we came into San Jose, we knew there might be some sort of greeting party put on by the parents," Mr Hodges remembers. "There were paper banners saying 'Welcome Back.' Moms were crying. Not sad crying, but happy crying."

Local television news crews showed up to cover the students' return.

"I remember one of them asking me what was one of the highlights of the trip," recalls Megan. "My quote was 'All of it.' It was just an amazing experience and so great to be with so many different kids from different backgrounds and that Mr Hodges was so willing to give his time and energy to take us on this life-changing trip."

"He showed us what we were capable of," says Linda. "We pushed ourselves so hard and he made it fun. At the end of the day we were laughing. I just appreciate him and all he did, and I know he's done it for so many others. I don't think he can truly know how life-changing he's been for hundreds and hundreds of kids."

In the junior high parking lot, Mr Hodges surveyed the scene. Beaming families. Kids bright with the potential they sensed inside themselves. A learning experience that no standardized test could ever capture.

Asked if he was aware at that point of the impact he'd made on those kids, Mr Hodges responded humbly, "No. I just provided them with an adventure. They've told me later on that it was a major event in their lives. I didn't plan it that way. I had just thought, 'What can we do? That looks fun.' And so that's what we did."

Postscript: Ed Hodges retired from teaching in the early 2000s, but continued to lead trips for students until 2020. He brought California history to life on backpacking trips into the Sierra, where students learned about the ill-fated Donner Party, a group of pioneers who were stranded after an early season storm blocked the wagon party's way out of the mountains and forced to resort to cannibalism. Always whimsical, Mr Hodges cut slices of baked Spam into the shape of gingerbread men and packaged them in small boxes reading "Emergency Rations for Students". He called them "Cannibal Cookies".

Adapted from reporting by Cordelia Zars

RIGHT The first few miles on Vancouver Island.

ALL IN THE FAMILY

📍 LOCATIONS   **MONASHEE MOUNTAINS, BC**

PEOPLE   **THE SCHAFFER FAMILY**

ACTIVITY   **SKIING, SNOWBOARDING**

ABOVE The reward of a cold beer after a day of walking up every slope you want to ski down.

All in the *Family*

FITZ CAHALL

Thwump. Thwump. Thwump.

The helicopter's blades tear through the winter air as the machine simultaneously banks and descends for landing. As the skids settle into a landing pad stomped out in the snow, the rotor wash animates tens of thousands of freshly fallen snowflakes into a momentary blizzard that stings exposed skin, sneaks down the back of jacket collars, and makes it difficult to breath. The paradox that every trip into the quiet depths of winter begins with a sudden flash of wondrous mechanical violence is never lost on me.

In a focused rush of unloading and loading, snapping latches, and shuffling of skis and gear, the occupants of the "bird" make room for their replacements. Smiles

(*no high fives around the helicopter please*) are exchanged. Thumbs up and the pilot throttles up, producing the second exfoliating cloud of snow that momentarily whites out the sky. It's the last we will see of it for five days.

A quick moment of awed silence as the physical surroundings are broken by a voice saturated with enthusiasm.

"Welcome to the Blanket," says Marty Schaffer with the psyche of a consummate ski bum, the assuredness of a seasoned mountain guide, and the jovial intensity of an entrepreneur who knows their product is about to blow someone's mind.

Behind him stands the "Eh" Frame, a steep, three-story A-frame cabin that serves as bunkhouse, living and dining quarters, and occasional late night discotheque. Beyond that, the Monashee Mountains, boasting one of the world's most reliable and deepest annual snowpacks, swell upward. To the north, the twin peaks of Castor and Pollux beckon; to the south the chalet's namesake, the Blanket Glacier, dominates the open alpine terrain rock outcroppings. Just behind the chalet, a set of 50-ft cliffs clustered with dollops of snow placed like giant ice creams beckon to be jumped. This is a backcountry skier or snowboarder's paradise. It's also the pioneering business that Marty was born into.

"I think if I knew what I know now, I would have went, 'I wonder if this is a good thing?'" remembers Marion Schaffer, Marty's mom, with a bit of a wink.

PIONEERS OF STOKE

In the 1980s and '90s, the Canadian province of British Columbia gained international fame for its heli-skiing operations. Guests were whisked to the day's set of runs by helicopter, plucked from the bottom of the mountain, and eventually returned back to luxury accommodations in the valley below. These operations brought in wealthy clients and money from around the globe.

Simultaneously, the region's backcountry ski lodges developed an alternative, cult following of die-hard skiers intent on chasing the best snow rather than being pampered. At the Blanket, every turn down the hill is earned by hiking up it. Climb mountains. Ski off them. Repeat. That is the mantra.

In 1986, when Marion and her husband Al purchased the Blanket Glacier Chalet, they were in the vanguard of skiing's future. Revelstoke, BC, was a struggling timber and railroad town, not the world-class ski destination it is today. With the era's long, straight, and skinny skis, powder skiing was the realm of experts. Avalanche safety and tactics for traveling safely through complex mountain terrain were nascent. Al and Marion dove in. With a small group of practitioners, they designed the earliest avalanche safety courses, which are now ubiquitous. At the chalet, they offered telemark ski touring and clinics to an ever-growing group of friends. In those early days, the experience at the chalet was rustic. Upon arrival, guests and owners alike had to dig the cabin out of the snow. Lanterns provided light. In the mornings, they formed a bucket brigade from the frozen lake, where a hole chopped into the ice provided fresh water for the day. They'd march uphill and trace squiggling turns down until their legs failed them.

GROWING A SPORT

"We were the first one in the area to really be granted that tenure, so it was very new," remembers Marion. "We were going to have to work our butts off to promote it and bring people on board."

It began with small classified ads in the back of ski mags and grew from there via return customers and word of mouth. Al helped author some of the earliest ski guiding protocols for the Association of Canadian Mountain Guides. Often the lodge sat empty, but slowly the ski industry moved toward the Schaffers' vision of skiing. Along the way, Al and Marion had Marty, and then his sister Heidi. The Schaffers hustled, and Marty and Heidi were in the mix right from the start. Marion likens it to growing up on a farm.

Christmas was always spent at the lodge among guests. Marty remembers visitors dressing as Santa and entering with snow on their heels to the delight of him and his sister. Heidi believed the caribou tracks to be those of St Nick's reindeer. The Schaffers' hard working, fun-loving brood, and their magical powder kingdom left an impression on guests, who returned year after year. Eventually Marty became their guide when he wasn't in school.

"I took the fast groups," remembers Marty. "There'd be a handful of folks that were fit and wanted to pound out vertical. I was excited. I was 13-years-old, breaking trail, and they just had full trust in me marching around in the mountains. Pretty early on I found out that fulfillment in the occupation isn't skiing powder, it's bringing the best out of people."

PASSING THE TORCH

The years passed. Marty and Heidi went to school, graduated, and started careers of their own. Marty started formally guiding, working for other outfits that had sprung up. In 2012, he started his own business, Canada Powder Guiding or, as it's better known, CAPOW! He brought a refreshing communicative style that treated skiers less like clients and more like friends.

OPPOSITE PAGE
Following the sun line in the backcountry of the Canadian Rockies.

RIGHT The remote Blanket Glacier Chalet—you're here until the helicopter comes to take you out again.

Marty developed camps and guided trips beyond his home turf of the Blanket.

Thirty years had passed since Al and Marion purchased the chalet. They continued the hard physical work of maintaining the lodge and guiding into their 60s. Their loyal clientele aged with them. The competition among the lodges had intensified, and the Blanket developed a reputation for mellow terrain as the community at large became obsessed with more aggressive, steep geography akin to what you'd find in a modern ski movie. Marion and Al hadn't just turned the Blanket into a viable business—they'd helped develop the entire industry of backcountry huts and guiding. Bigger, corporate interests were starting to take note, snapping up mom and pop lodges as founders looked for a way to retire. Now, that industry seemed to be leaving the older Schaffers behind.

Marty could see his parents needed help and that the lodge required some physical updates to keep up with the times and guest expectations. With some trepidation, Marty stepped in.

"From cleaning the outhouse to chopping all the wood for next season to cleaning up the whole lodge for the summer, there's a lot of shitty stuff that goes on behind the scenes. It's not all skiing pow and getting to hang out with people," says Marty. Helicopter fuel bills, future renovation plans, and staff payroll all have to be balanced on a shoestring budget.

Heidi, who'd gone on to become a chef, returned as well, to create the dining experience, which is unparalleled for an A-frame deep inside the Canadian wilderness. Marty revisited the terrain, scouting new zones in search of steep terrain peppered with cliffs. He pushed farther into their tenure, figuring out ways to connect features into day-long tours that would leave guests smiling and exhausted. He invited pro-skiers for clinics. In the summers, with the cabin snow-free, he put in long hours remodeling the chalet, adding running water, and installing a small hydro-electric and solar power system for electricity. He revamped marketing materials to cater to the Instagram-savvy set. With his parents as sounding boards, Marty hustled to bring the Blanket back into skiing's forefront.

THE NEXT CHAPTER

"We are very proud of both of them," says Marion. "But sometimes I wonder for Marty, 'Has he taken on too much?' He's making an amazing product and it's totally different from what we did which it should be. It's hard to watch how hard he's working though."

Despite all the physical effort long days of skiing require, they're the easy part of the business. The second shift begins after dinner when Marty goes to work coordinating guides, resupplies, and future bookings. Days off can easily become days on when another guide is sick or injured. He's part chief operations officer and part chief entertainer. The family's charisma is part of what keeps people coming back.

What his parents had built here was special and Marty sensed that the younger set of skiers didn't mind using an outhouse or foregoing a few days of Internet connectivity. They were after experience and connection. The Blanket could provide.

Almost a decade later, their efforts have paid off. Today, the Blanket is always booked. CAPOW! employs a team of guides. Marty met his wife there and there will be another generation of Schaffers spending Christmas at the lodge.

"Like a lot of things in life, it's not how badly you want something, it's how badly you're willing to suffer for it. And that's where a lot of the fulfillment comes from," says Marty.

Marion and Al's pride is apparent. Al often meets guests at the takeoff area, chitchatting with them and catching up with the guides even though he's retired. After all, this is an idea and business that's carried through generations and defined a family. Marty's enthusiasm allowed his parents' dream to survive while realizing his own. The rest of us are just lucky enough to enjoy the fruits of those labors.

Marty sensed that the younger set of skiers didn't mind using an outhouse or foregoing a few days of Internet connectivity. They were after experience and connection.

Paul's *Boots*

FITZ CAHALL

The August heat in The Dirtbag Diaries' second-story Seattle office made it hard to concentrate on creative work. Napping or a quick dip in the lake sounded much better. Then the phone rang. I can't remember who answered, but the next thing I remember was our team of creatives huddled around a speakerphone listening to a woman's voice. It was American, tinged with a subtle Aussie accent, emanating across an ocean from the tiny town of Ipswich, Queensland.

There are the stories we tell. And then there are the stories you have to tell. From the urgency and

conviction M'Lynn spoke with, we could tell what she was about to tell us fell into the latter. She had an idea. She thought we could help.

A BIG HEART
M'Lynn's husband, Paul, was a big guy with a quick wit, a kind heart, and a deep passion for the outdoors. They met online in the kinder, gentler era of 1990s Internet message boards. M'Lynn had come to visit Paul in Australia and ended up staying for good. When Paul was 42, doctors diagnosed his mother with Parkinson's. He nursed her for four years, until she passed. Then his

As a community, could we get Paul's spirit across the entire length of the trail?

PAUL'S BOOTS

📍 LOCATIONS	**APPALACHIAN TRAIL, USA**
PEOPLE	**PAUL AND M'LYNN**
ACTIVITY	**HIKING**

ABOVE The Real Hiking Viking took the boots on the trail whatever the weather.

father developed Alzheimer's. The gaps between Paul's hiking trips to the Australian bush grew bigger. His passion for them, though, remained unchanged.

Paul's own health began to deteriorate. By 2014, he'd suffered a series of debilitating heart attacks. Even as his body failed him, he started packing for the epic journey he'd always dreamed of one day completing—the 2,190-mile long Appalachian Trail (AT), the revered long-distance hiking trail that snakes up the USA's east coast. Traversing 14 states, most thru-hikers cover the distance in five to seven months, walking an average of 15–20 miles a day over roots, rocks, and occasionally smooth single track. Paul organized his food and gear. At night, he'd recount to M'Lynn all he'd learned in his online research. His heart no longer allowed him to walk much farther than the end of his block, but his

soul was ready to go. Next to a full backpack, he left three sets of polished hiking boots.

In July 2015, Paul passed away. He was 53 years old. In the midst of her grief, M'Lynn had an idea for one final gift to her husband – to get his boots out on the AT.

"I have three sets of well-cared-for boots size 12-13 that someone could have," she said, hoping that someone might take them out for a weekend trip or two. "All I ask in return is a photo of them on the trail."

She had the sense that we might be able to connect her to the community of American hikers. We immediately got to work with a bigger goal—could we get Paul's boots the entire length of the Appalachian Trail?

THE GREAT MIGRATION

Since the first documented thru-hike in 1936, a complete journey across the AT has had cultural cache. The Appalachian Trail Conservancy, the body in charge of maintaining this National Scenic Trail, has registered more than 20,000 complete thru-hikes. Today, a typical year sees more than 3,000 people set off across the forested hills and mountains in the hopes of reaching the other side. The grind of miles isn't for everyone. Overuse injuries aren't uncommon and six months of sleeping on the ground can prove too much for some people. Less than a quarter will complete the route, but everyone gets a taste of the magic of this pilgrimage. Many thousands more pick sections of the trail to cover in shorter periods of time. While the trail traverses dozens of distinct wilderness routes, thru-hiking experiences are a communal one, with friendships

LEFT From Katahdin, the AT stretches south and west, overlooking Baxter State Park.

forged via shared steps and rainy evenings squeezed into the 250 rustic, three-sided shelters that punctuate the miles. Fate, circumstance, and fellow hikers bestow whimsical trail names on each hiker. If you decide that you're going to carry a 10-lb cast-iron pan on the outside of your pack, there's a good chance you'll be christened Skillet for your commitment to well-seasoned cookware.

While most thru-hikers skew to just-out-of-university 20-somethings, the trail meets people at every stage of life. Intrepid families have hiked it, and it's not uncommon to see someone in their mid-70s working their way over the tangle of roots and rocks that define much of the walking. By the end, everyone smells. Most are smiling.

In late February, the first wave of northbound hikers converge on Springer Mountain in Georgia to kick off the season. That winter, we broadcast M'Lynn's wish on social media and our podcast: would anyone be willing to take Paul's boots for a walk on the AT? As a community, could we get Paul's spirit across the entire length of the trail? We had no idea what to expect, but M'Lynn's request spread via social media and message boards. By the end of January, we'd received more than 400 responses. College students about to graduate and looking for their first adventure. Twenty- and thirty-somethings looking for a path through life, but struggling to figure out where they fit. There were 40-year-olds trying to maintain a connection to the outdoors in the midst of family and career. Fifty-year-olds chasing their teenagers down the trail, and 70-year-olds looking to wrap up unfinished dreams.

"Trail magic" is the overwhelming sense that karma will provide for those who give it their all. Today, that ethos manifests as freshly cooked meals that appear at road crossings. A ride to town shows up right when you need it. It's not unheard of to stumble across a cooler of beer and ice cream or a local flipping burgers on a portable grill. There is a prevailing sense that while everyone has to hike their hike, nobody hikes alone. Three-thousand miles away in our Seattle office, we could tell we were on the receiving end of a thunderous outburst of trail magic.

THE HANDOFF

By late February, the boots were racing south through Virginia on the back of "The Real Hiking Viking". In the midst of the first-ever winter thru-hike of the Appalachian Trail, the Viking, as we came to know him, retired as a Marine sniper at 29 after two tours in Iraq.

ABOVE Paul's boots start the AT at Springer Mountain, GA, with Daddy Long Legs.

RIGHT The boots enjoy the sunset at Twin Lakes with Katahdin in the background.

A few years earlier, he stumbled into the AT community while working as a marketing intern on a gear booth at a hiking festival. The next winter he quit college and started walking, completing the AT, Pacific Crest Trail, and Continental Divide Trail—the "triple crown" of American hiking—in blazing fast times. He returned to complete the masochistic act of walking through the New England woods in sub-zero temperatures and blizzards. As he carried the boots, he sent M'Lynn and us notes and photos. We built a friendship.

To the south, with a second pair of boots, "Daddy Long Legs" started the journey north from Springer Mountain. Suffering from epilepsy, Daddy Long Legs was setting out on his second attempt at a thru-hike—

he'd made it more than two-thirds of the way the previous year before circumstances forced him to stop. Though he'd had a seizure only weeks earlier, Paul's boots were the nudge he needed to give it a second go.

"I got tired of being told no, of being told what I can't do," he told us with deep conviction.

In North Carolina, Grace set out on her first big backpacking trip with the third pair of 4½-lb boots tied to her pack. "Cubby and CoMoMdo", a daughter-mother team, took over. Two years earlier, CoMoMdo had pulled her family out of everyday life after another daughter experienced aftershocks from the trauma of a sexual assault. She helped her family heal on the trail.

Young couples, families, and friends pushed the boots through the rolling hills of the Mid-Atlantic. By early summer, it was clear Paul's boots had a chance of making it all the way north to Mount Katahdin in Maine, the trail's end. "Two Pennies", a teacher from Colorado who had lost two brothers to a genetic heart disorder, took the boots into Vermont. Doctors outfitted him with an internal defibrillator with electrodes wired directly to his heart in case it stopped. Along with the boots, he carried two pennies that had belonged to his brothers. He weaved through Vermont's famous Green Mountains connecting with other hikers who had carried the boots. By August, the boots had made it past New Hampshire's rugged summits.

M'Lynn, accompanied by Paul's younger brother, Arthur, made the long journey from Australia to northern Maine. Arthur would carry his brother's boots the final leg to the end. Isaiah, my coworker who spent a good chunk of the summer filming the boots progress, and I flew in from Seattle. The Viking flew in to surprise M'Lynn.

At the airport, we all exchanged hugs. We had some boots to catch before the last rugged climb up the flanks of Katahdin. The King family from Rhode Island had hiked the boots north to the base of the mountain. That night, M'Lynn cooked a spaghetti feast for us all. A little more than a year after his passing, she and Arthur shared stories of Paul. From the window of the guesthouse, we could see clouds gathering on Katahdin's crest.

The first hint of fall snuck into the late summer morning. In a few weeks' time, northern Maine's forests would be a patchwork blaze of reds, yellows, and oranges. Arthur, the Viking, Isaiah, the King family and myself gathered at the trailhead.

FINAL SUMMIT
The anchor of the trail's northern terminus, Katahdin is arguably the AT's greatest summit. It rises up like a dragon's back above Maine's famed lakes. Granite talus falls aways from its sheer sides like scales. From Katahdin Stream Campground, the Hunt Trail gathers steam, driving upward for 4,000ft in just under six

miles. Three miles in, hikers encounter the Gateway, a steep scramble between and over granite boulders—iron rods, drilled into the granite, help the scramble over the steepest slabs. Arthur paused as the rest of the group continued upward, the exertion and jet lag momentarily overwhelming him, his legs cramping. We sat in silence, as Arthur gathered his strength and resolved to push through the 500ft of boulder hopping.

Atop the Gateway, hikers crest onto Katahdin's magnificent, Tolkienesque plateau. Hard winters stunt and twist trees, before the trail eventually crosses a field of dull gray talus, gently rising to the terminus. Together, our small crew reconvened and Arthur, catching a second wind and energized by the enthusiasm and high fives of fellow hikers recognizing the boots strapped to his pack, trudged the last mile to Katahdin's summit.

Clouds swept over us, occasionally parting to provide views into the thick forests, lakes, and rivers to the north, the sheer walls of the mountain's north side falling away 3,000ft below us. Arthur took the final few steps to the large brown sign that marks the end of the AT. He stood smiling, drenched in sweat, but happy. Connected by the laces, his brother's boots draped around his neck.

"When I was cramping, I could hear him in the back of my head, saying, 'Arthur, you have to do it. You have to get there,'" he recalled.

We laughed. We shed tears. We had been strangers, but that day we all shared a powerful moment. To the uninitiated, spending months on the AT might seem like a form of escapism, but those who walk it know it as a place of connection. Eventually the clouds blew in,

tightening around the summit. Accepting that it was time to go, we turned to slowly make our way back down the mountain. Hours later, we emerged out of the trees exhausted and dehydrated, but still smiling. M'Lynn was waiting at the trailhead with snacks and water, beaming. She hugged each of us.

"Thank you. Your time with people is short and our time here is limited," she said. "I lost sight of that with Paul. We both did. It's really important to get out there and do things that feed your soul, to do things that make you say this is what life's all about."

We nodded in agreement. That night, we all celebrated around a campfire, tiny embers drifting upward and fading into a night sky alive with laughter. I added another log to the fire. No one wanted the magic to end. In the morning, we each went our separate ways. M'Lynn reconnected with her stateside family with the help of Arthur. The Viking returned to the trail. A few weeks later, Daddy Long Legs made it to Katahdin with the final set of boots. That summer, the boots covered almost 3,000 miles. To this day, via social

media and text, I keep track of the dozens of people who helped carry Paul's boots. One pair went to M'Lynn's sister in California. One set went off on the Pacific Crest Trail a year later, and the final pair made it to a research station in Antarctica before we lost track. Presumably, the boots are still out there, somewhere, headed to the next adventure.

"When I was cramping, I could hear him in the back of my head, saying, 'Arthur, you have to do it. You have to get there.'"

LEFT While many miles of the AT unfurl under a canopy of trees, the sweeping vistas offer an open-sky respite.

RIGHT Two pairs of boots at the summit of Katahdin with the King family, Fitz, Paul's brother Arthur, Isaiah, and The Real Hiking Viking.

Widge

FITZ CAHALL

When Jonah left to sail around the world, Widge arrived on Jamie's doorstep at just the right moment.

"When you're scared to move forward, you need someone to give you a little nudge," says Jonah Manning. "You could call it support, but really it's a bit of a shove. Widge was certainly that for me."

Jonah was 15 when he met Widge in rural South Carolina. Jonah was living the high school years of Americana lore—top-50 country songs playing on his truck's radio, late-night partying, jockeying for love. The two shared a passion for hunting—Widge's given name was Widgeon, a type of duck. Sensing there was more to life than living out the lyrics of country songs, Jonah enrolled in college in Tennessee while Widge stayed

behind. But Jonah found himself right back in the social dynamic he'd tried to leave.

At 19, Jonah took a gap year from college to travel out west. Widge jumped into the packed truck and they followed a couple of friends out to Jackson Hole, WY, for the summer. Famed for the sweeping vista of the Tetons and winding rivers that define western Wyoming, Jackson Hole is a land of opportunity to young adventurers. They slept beneath stars and followed dirt roads deeper into forests. That summer, Jonah worked early mornings until noon, then they'd spend the afternoons and evenings riding ribbons of singletrack

WIDGE

📍 LOCATIONS	**ALL OVER USA**	
PEOPLE	**JONAH MANNING AND JAMIE WOOD**	
ACTIVITY	**HIKING, SKIING**	

ABOVE A dog's life—always out in front.

in the Tetons with Widge running out ahead, his energy and enthusiasm contagious to those who shared the trail with him.

LONG-DISTANCE FRIENDSHIP
Jonah heard about the Appalachian Trail, the iconic thru-hike stretching from northern Georgia to Mount Katahdin in Maine, and the idea took hold. After regrouping from the Wyoming summer, the duo started hiking from Springer Mountain, GA.

"It was more or less analogous to what we thought we wanted to get out of life—simple living, lots of hiking, and a fair bit of suffering," Jonah recalls. "It was a quintessential experience where you find the things that are really important to you."

As spring gave way to summer, the duo blazed north as the East Coast's hardwood forests leafed out, enveloping them in what hikers lovingly refer to as "the Green Tunnel". A thru-hike along the AT is far from a solitary experience. It's become a pilgrimage of sorts for young people, something to do after college or as a reset between jobs in your 20s. Widge, now slightly older, fitted right in among the thousands of hikers who attempt a thru-hike each year. He became a legend for stealing people's sleeping pads in the old lean-tos that dot the trail every 20 miles or so. When they stood atop Katahdin five months later, it was a crowning achievement for Jonah and Widge, tinged with the realization that they had made a life beyond the horizon of their youth.

Jonah decided to continue his studies in Montana. Friends from Tennessee followed and moved in with Jonah and Widge. Enamored with the stories of the AT, two of these friends, Jamie and Rob decided to make the journey. That spring, Jonah and Widge joined them for the first few days on the trail, but when it came time to head back to school, Jonah left and Widge kept walking with Jamie and Rob.

"When I left him on the trail, he never looked back," remembers Jonah. "He was just going forward."

WIDE OPEN
Through their shared adventures, Widge's close friends developed a sense of direction in life. Jamie joined the elite search rescue team responsible for finding lost hikers and plucking injured climbers from Yosemite Valley's sheer cliffs. Rob took a job at the National Outdoor Leadership School. Widge migrated back to Montana as Jonah finished his degree. As the years

passed, Widge grew comfortable couch surfing between friends' homes and vehicles. He watched them grow, follow love to new homes, and realize grand visions. When Jonah left to sail around the world, Widge arrived on Jamie's doorstep at just the right moment. In her late 20s, she'd left the park service and moved to Alaska.

"I kind of needed Widge around," remembers Jamie. "I'd fallen in love and left everything behind for that. I was leaving climbing for a more stable life and having Widge there made that journey so much easier."

Jamie always had a friend to coax her out into the mountains for a trail run. Even as wisps of gray colored his whiskers, Widge learned to backcountry ski, marching up the steep flanks of the mountains surrounding Anchorage alongside her. Known for deep powder, the mountains in southern Alaska are a bucket list destination for skiers. Many partake in the guided heli-skiing outfits that shuttle skiers to the top of the peaks, but locals and diehards walk up these steep mountains to ski what they climbed. As his fellow skiers peeled off climbing skins atop a peak after climbing several thousand feet, Widge approached each descent in his own unique way—head first and on his back. As his friends dropped in, Widge flipped over, letting gravity pull him down as he gained speed until he crashed into a cloud of powder. Then he'd resume swimming downhill on all fours, diving down into the snow and then back up to grab a breath as his friends whooped.

To this day, Jamie keeps a photo of herself and Widge. They're in the Chugach Mountains above Anchorage in the midst of a 26-mile trail run. It's above the treeline, with clear lines of sight between peaks and valleys.

"Widge is just running wide open in front of me the whole time," Jamie says as she describes the photo. "He was always running wide open, just so exuberant and happy with life, so that was always my vision of him."

A SLOWER PACE
Years passed. In her early 30s, Jamie had completed nursing school and her then-husband entered the clinical rotations of medical school which meant near constant travel and time away from the open spaces Widge had spent his life chasing. Old age found Widge. He could no longer run "wide open".

Jamie had grown up on a farm in northern Alabama, a place that after all her travels and adventures still filled the place inside her heart known as home. Her father,

Jimmy, was going through a difficult time, getting on in his years and still running the 3,800-acre holding, with its fields and herd of cattle. He could use someone to walk with. After thousands of miles running and hiking across the Appalachian Mountains, the open spaces of the West and the Alaskan wilds, Widge now moved at the relaxed pace of old age. It made sense for him to live out this next chapter on the farm, so Jamie said goodbye.

Together, Jimmy and Widge tended to the farm in a pickup truck. Each day, they'd stop to have lunch in the same spot and enjoy the sunshine together, two friends embracing a moment of quiet.

One day, in the midst of their routine, Jimmy and Widge were walking down the long gravel driveway that connects the family home to the highway, when Widge lay down and died. Jimmy scooped Widge up and carried him to a small hill overlooking white and green rows of cotton growing beneath the Alabama sun. He marked Widge's final resting place with a stone.

"I'd never had a dog," says Jimmy. "I mean, there were dogs that used to stay outside on the farm, but I'd never had a dog that rode with me, that traveled with me. I'm having a hard time talking about it now. I really do miss him. He's a sweet dog."

BEST FRIEND TO MANY
It's hard not to wonder what went through Widge's mind in those final moments. The feel of an open truck window headed west. The hum of summer cicadas on a quiet stretch of the Appalachian Trail. The sting of cold powder on an Alaskan peak. Sunshine at the perfect lunch spot. Maybe the voices of the people he'd cared for and who'd cared for him flowed together into one wide-open feeling of home. We all need a nudge. Widge had given many.

"Growing up on a farm, you know every tree, ditch, and blade of grass. I kept traveling trying to find that same feeling in all these different places. They were all beautiful, but nothing ever felt like home," says Jamie, who ultimately returned to take over the family business. "The journey to get here was pretty circuitous, and I'm so grateful it was. I probably wouldn't have taken such an extended journey to get here if Widge hadn't been there. I always had a running buddy. I always had someone to ride in the truck with me. He was an important part of life—a little, furry, brown guardian angel."

RIGHT Canine walking companions can give just as much support as human ones.

PREVIOUS PAGE
A pause at the peak.

AMONG THE BIG TREES

📍 LOCATIONS   **INDEX, WA**

PEOPLE   **FITZ CAHALL**

ACTIVITY   **CLIMBING**

ABOVE Fitz looking out from Upper Town Wall in Index, WA.

Among the *Big Trees*

FITZ CAHALL

RIGHT Index has slowly become an excellent destination for climbing.

Over the last 25 years, I've walked the trail to the Upper Town Wall more times than I can remember. Across the train tracks where forest joins the base of the lower walls, the trail climbs steeply via a series of switchbacks through Douglas firs, as granite walls soar above the sleepy hamlet of Index, WA. A staple of Pacific Northwest forest, in good years these trees grow about two feet a year. They might be 50ft taller than when I first walked through decades ago.

An hour's drive from Seattle, Index marks the Cascades' transition from foothills to mountains. The rarely climbed Mount Index broods across the valley,

impressive but brushy and broken. The Skykomish River pours steady and cold from the mountains beyond. The speckled granite on this side of the valley has captured local climbers' attention from as far back as the 1950s. It was the perfect training ground for the North Cascades and Yosemite to the south.

When I first arrived here as a wide-eyed teenager in the late 1990s, a busy weekend meant a handful of climbers gathered around a few oft-climbed classics just a brief walk from the parking lot. Freight trains rumbled by, rattling the nerves of the climbers clinging to the small, tenuous holds that define the movement here. The place

had an air of mystery, almost like an old country estate that had fallen into disrepair. Old bolts and rusting pitons proved that people clearly once gathered here, but had moved on—leaving the forest and its moss, ferns, and blackberry bushes to reclaim sections of the walls. Information was sparse and the vegetation persistent. Visiting climbers did a few of the obvious well-traveled classics and then quickly moved on to other Pacific Northwest destinations like Squamish or Smith Rock. They understandably weren't interested in reclaiming routes from time and the forest.

Slowly, Index went through a rebirth. By the mid-2000s, the walls began to stir excitement in a new generation of Seattle climbers. Information about routes became more readily shared and available over the Internet. At less traveled cliffs, motivated locals reclaimed and replaced aging bolts on the previous generations' efforts, adding their own new routes along the way. Hundreds of worthy climbs emerged from beneath the moss and lichen. Slowly, Index became the excellent, if not quite world-class, rock climbing destination it is today.

These days, on busy weekends, cars spill outward from the cliff's parking lot along the narrow, two-lane country road. Laughter echoes through the forest and, on a summer evening, the most accessible crags are equal parts social event and workout. There are more devoted locals to keep the moss at bay through regular climbing and the occasional scrub and trim. Visiting climbers stay for a week or two rather than a day. The train still rumbles by at terrifying speeds, but the mansion no longer feels haunted.

Some of the older generation, which surprisingly I am now a part of, occasionally lament the crowds. In many ways, what's happened at Index is a microcosm of what's happened in the greater outdoor adventure community. No longer fringe, these pursuits have attracted a broader, more diverse, and definitively larger portion of the culture at large. The outdoor industry likes to tout the fact that recreation contributes more to the American economy than the fossil fuel industry. A generation of young parents will turn to our forests and open spaces as outdoor classrooms and backyards as they raise children. Being outside is no longer synonymous with solitude. Change is inevitable, even if it's hard to see it happening in the moment. It's difficult to recognize that the trees have grown around you.

As I plod up the steep switchbacks, sweat gathers on my brow and I fall into a familiar pace. The big trees obscure the 600-ft tall Upper Town Wall, standing proud above the valley below. I've made this approach as a youngster with brand-new gear, ambition, and barely enough skills to stay alive. I learned and traveled widely, and returned again and again, looking for more difficult routes up the wall, as the classics began to feel like reliable afternoon jaunts. I grew cocky enough to eschew the rope completely. That swagger ebbed, leaving behind a quiet confidence and love for the shared experience of trying hard with close friends. Today at 45, I'm not as ambitious, bold, or strong as those former selves. Objectively, the routes aren't as difficult or mentally involved. Subjectively, they don't feel that way. The rope is mandatory. On a level, I'm less of a climber, but I am happier, calmer, and maybe even a little more grateful to be here. In my ever-evolving life, Index feels like an old friend with whom I fall easily back into conversations from months or even years before.

A DIFFERENT SPOTLIGHT

I've watched my friends and peers realize incredible dreams. Some of them reached the top of their craft, authoring improbable lines up remote mountains and locating the edges of human endurance. Others made careers documenting the world's wildest places. The road trip became global. We carried home stories; some of us even became famous. Others never returned. The greater culture turned its attention to our rare little community that put experience ahead of stability and comfort. The horizon grew outward. The spotlight glowed bright enough that filmmakers and photographers recorded achievements for the world to see. With a few clicks of the TV remote, the faces of friends from old campfires blaze to life on the screen. Occasionally, a fall breeze on pine trees will trigger a memory and I'll chuckle at how humbly this all began. We were young. Climbing was magic. There were routes to do and campfires to share. Not much else mattered.

These days, when friends swing through Seattle to stay for a night before catching an international flight, I make sure my kids pepper them with questions about their journeys across the globe—about their experiences and all the incredible things they've seen. They pull out iPhones and the kids flip through frames.

The next morning, they catch a flight off to some exotic place. I make lunches for the boys, walk them to school, and then ride my bike three-and-a-half miles to work. I'm glad my children get to meet the people I shared big days in the mountains with when I was younger. I'm glad they see people carving an alternative path through life—finding a calling and growing to meet it.

If I look back on the last 12 years, I'm often surprised that I didn't end up on their trajectory. Certainly, I had those opportunities. There were years where it seemed like my bag was always packed. I oscillated between here and there and back again. Often I found myself wanting to be somewhere else.

An inner voice, quiet and steady, called me in a different direction, one that I struggled against at first. Seattle had been a base camp for my 20s and 30s. Maybe what I needed was a home. Something inside of me knew that to become strong, I needed to grow down. Roots connect the tree to the forest, and I needed to be a part of something bigger than myself. So, I grew down, looking for nourishment, for stillness, for presence, for home.

★ ★ ★

Last summer, my youngest son Wiley was as content searching for slugs and lizards as he was climbing. On a late summer day, the first bigleaf maple leaves turned banana-peel yellow, and Wiley had a vision.

Belay on?

Belay on.

Climbing.

He scampered up the granite wall with intent. Should climbing speak to him, I imagine he would be quite good, but that day I could tell the rope was the means to a different end. Forty feet up, the branch of the maple tree tickled the cliff side. Level with the branch of golden leaves, Wiley asked me to hold him with the rope. I took tight as he stretched out and plucked the yellow leaf. He paused, examining it, then let go. As the leaf fell to earth, it drifted back and forth on the nearly imperceptible breeze. I watched. Wiley sent another leaf aloft.

"One more?" he asked from above.

"One more," I nodded. The leaf fell, catching a shaft of sunlight.

Later, with only a few pitches completed, we packed up the climbing gear, exited the woods, and walked along the railroad tracks. The boys balanced on the rails. We picked blackberries before stopping at the tiny general store where they chose ice creams from the freezer. We made our way to the large swimming hole, taking the last plunge of the season. After the long summer, the cold waters of the Skykomish were in no particular rush. The boys cannonballed into the deep clear water of the eddy. A few surprised salmon skittered off the bottom of the pool and disappeared upstream in a flash of red, waiting for the next big rain to replenish the tiny side streams in which they were born. I am always amazed by their specificity. After years of traveling the ocean, the exact combination of nutrients, water, and location remains burned into their being. That sense of home powers the survival of the species.

A few days later, school would begin. Another Index season would pass, but for that moment, the boys and I basked in a good sugar buzz, the dichotomy of cold water and fading heat, and a well-executed cannonball. The moment felt recognizable, even innate. It felt like home.

ROOTED AND GROWING

In my 20s, I needed climbing to grow as a person. I poured my heart into it and, subsequently, it taught me a great deal beyond the craft. I learned that I felt the most successful when I made myself vulnerable to failure. Through practice, I understood that there is a big difference between cutting your losses and giving up. I grew to embrace maximal effort and the presence it demanded. Growth always occurred at the horizon of my skill set.

Now, I find growth in raising Tep and Wiley. I find it in my relationship with Becca. I find it in my friendships. I find it in my work and creative collaborations. Those climbing lessons became a foundation that I've built from. Marching upward toward the Upper Town Wall, it's clear I still love it, but some of the urgency has slipped away. I no longer need to push myself to enjoy myself.

I pull ropes from the bag, slightly musty from the summer's humidity. The sun creeps above the horizon. Light spills over the mountains into the valley. I flake the ropes.

The climbing at Index is hard to explain. The holds are often small, and the movements cryptic. It's precarious, but through the years I've grown comfortable with the insecurity. It's a place where technique is more important than power, which is good for a middle-aged dad relying on muscle memory.

I work upward on a route that I've done dozens of times.

I get to the top and descend again.

I'm eye level with the treetops. The big firs sway, pushed and pulled by a summer breeze. I think of the roots that hold these trees in place. So often, I think of these big trees as fixed, still, immovable objects, but from this perspective the paradox is clear: it's possible to simultaneously be grounded and dynamic.

I keep climbing.

Below, the ice-blue Skykomish pours from the Cascades. The train rolls by, churning across America with startling velocity. On the other side of the valley, the hulking mass of Mount Index looms.

After 20 years, I have yet to tire of this view. I doubt I will. I feel that the range of ideas I pursue has expanded, but the geographic footprint I inhabit has narrowed. These days, I don't need climbing to be a crucible for growth. I need it to be a connection to places I love and the community I've come from. Most of all, I need it because it's fun and fun things are always worth doing.

I keep climbing, and then something happens.

All the years, all the moves, blur together and for a second I can't remember where I am on this particular route, or even what particular route I'm on, or how old I am. Whether I'm the wild-eyed 19-year-old with a headful of dreams; or the slightly nervous 27-year-old about to embark on the adventure of a lifetime; or the middle-aged dad who finally understands the power of home. I am all these people at once. It is complete presence. I've stopped looking forward or backward. I've grown down, rooted into the wonderful network of moments that define my life.

I pause, smiling. I feel at home. Then I keep climbing.

Index

Picture Credits

The publisher would like to thank the following for their kind permission to reproduce their photographs:

(Key: a-above; b-below/bottom; c-centre; f-far; l-left; r-right; t-top)

1 Jason Hummel. 2-3 Alexa Flower. 4-5 Zoya Lynch. 7 Alamy Stock Photo: Realy Easy Star / Roberto Carnevali. **8-9 Austin Siadak. 10 Jason Hummel:** (c). **11 Greg Balkin:** (r). **12-13 Jesse Roesler Credo Nonfiction. 14 Greg Balkin. 15 Andy Earl:** (tr). **16-17 Austin Siadak. 18 Ryan Salm:** (t). **18-212 Dorling Kindersley:** Timba Smits (background behind maps). **19 Getty Images:** George Rose (c). **21 Ryan Salm. 22-23 Ryan Salm. 24 Peter and Kathy Holcombe:** (t). **25 Peter and Kathy Holcombe:** (clb, cra, crb). **26-27 Peter and Kathy Holcombe. 28 Peter and Kathy Holcombe:** (b). **31 Peter and Kathy Holcombe:** (b). **32 Cordelia Zars:** (t). **33 Cordelia Zars:** (t). **34 Cordelia Zars:** (t). **35 Cordelia Zars:** (tr). **36-37 Cordelia Zars:** (bc). **37 Cordelia Zars:** (tl, tr, br). **38 Zach Clanton:** (l). **40 Colette McInerney:** (clb). **41 Zach Clanton. 42 Dreamstime.com:** Alexey Poprotskiy (tl). **43 Jan Novak:** (tr). **44 Alamy Stock Photo:** Dave Stamboulis (t). **45 Brendan Leonard:** (cr). **48 Ashlee Langholz:** (cl). **49 Katie Baird:** (t). **50 Avi Stachenfeld:** (b). **52-53 Ashlee Langholz. 54 Austin Siadak. 55 Alamy Stock Photo:** Celso Diniz (t). **56-57 Alexa Flower:** (bl). **57 DDTB:** (tl). **58 DDTB:** (t). **59 Alamy Stock Photo:** All Canada Photos / Ryan Creary (r). **60-61 Mikey Schaeffer. 62 Grant Myrdal:** (cla). **63 Alamy Stock Photo:** Jenna V. Genio (t). **64 Grant Myrdal. 66-67 Alamy Stock Photo:** VWPics / Terray Sylvester. **68 Gregg Bleakney:** (cla). **69 Gregg Bleakney:** (t). **70 Gregg Bleakney:** (bl). **71 Gregg Bleakney:** (t). **72 Gregg Bleakney. 73 Gregg Bleakney:** (bl). **74 Ashlee Langholz:** (t). **75 Ashlee Langholz:** (cra). **76-77 Ashlee Langholz. 80-81 Ashlee Langholz. 82 Mikey Schaeffer:** (t). **83 Mikey Schaeffer:** (cra). **84-85 Mikey Schaeffer. 87 Austin Siadak. 88 Jesse Roesler Credo Nonfiction:** (cl). **89 Jesse Roesler Credo Nonfiction:** (t). **90-91 Jesse Roesler Credo Nonfiction:** (tl). **92-93 Jesse Roesler Credo Nonfiction. 94 Jesse Roesler Credo Nonfiction:** (t). **95 Jesse Roesler Credo Nonfiction:** (b). **96 Shutterstock.com:** Tom Robertson (bl). **97 Mikey Schaeffer:** (t). **98-99 Mikey Schaeffer. 101 Mikey Schaeffer:** (tr). **102 Kat Cannell:** (cl). **103 Alamy Stock Photo:** Jesse Thornton (t). **104-105 Kat Cannell:** (tl). **106-107 Kat Cannell. 109 Shutterstock.com:** Florence-Joseph McGinn. **110 Andy Earl:** (t). **111 Andy Earl:** (cla). **112 Andy Earl:** (t). **113 Andy Earl:** (b). **114-115 Shutterstock.com:** Jon Bilous. **116 Andy Earl:** (t, bl, br). **117 Andy Earl:** (tr). **118-119 Andy Earl:** (tl). **120-121 Jason Hummel. 122 Jason Hummel:** (cra). **123 Jason Hummel:** (t). **124 Jason Hummel:** (t). **125 Jason Hummel:** (r). **126 Jason Hummel:** (tl). **128 Greg Balkin:** (cla). **129 Greg Balkin:** (t). **130 Greg Balkin:** (t). **131 Greg Balkin:** (b). **132 Greg Balkin. 133 Greg Balkin:** (t). **134-135 Greg Balkin. 136 Euan Fraser:** (t). **137 Euan Fraser:** (cr). **138-139 Bobby Biskupiak. 140 Euan Fraser:** (b). **142 Becca Cahall:** (cl). **143 Ashlee Langholz:** (t). **144 Becca Cahall:** (tl). **145 Ashlee Langholz:** (b). **146 Ashlee Langholz. 148 Andrew Burton:** (t). **149 Alamy Stock Photo:** Ryan McGinnis (cra). **150 Andrew Burton. 152-153 Andrew Burton. 154 Nate Ptacek:** (tl). **155 Nate Ptacek:** (t). **157 Nate Ptacek:** (r). **158 Nate Ptacek:** (t). **159 Nate Ptacek:** (b). **160-161 Nate Ptacek. 162 Nate Ptacek:** (b). **163 Nate Ptacek:** (br). **164 Alexa Flower. 166 Alamy Stock Photo:** Image Professionals GmbH / Uli Wiesmeier (cl). **167 Ali Vignini. 168-169 Jody MacDonald. 170 Jason Hummel:** (clb). **171 Jason Hummel:** (t). **172-173 Jason Hummel. 174 Jason Hummel:** (t). **175 Getty Images / iStock:** E+ / franckreporter. **176-177 Jason Hummel:** (tl). **178 Jody MacDonald:** (t). **179 Jody MacDonald:** (cra). **180 Jody MacDonald:** (t). **182-183 Jody MacDonald. 184 Ed Hodges:** (clb). **185 Ed Hodges:** (t). **186 Ed Hodges:** (t). **187 Ed Hodges:** (br). **188 Ed Hodges:** (tl). **189 Ed Hodges. 190 Ed Hodges:** (l). **191 Ed Hodges:** (br). **192 Zoya Lynch:** (t). **193 Mikey Schaeffer:** (cr). **194 Zoya Lynch:** (t). **195 Mikey Schaeffer:** (br). **197 Zoya Lynch:** (t). **198 Becca Cahall:** (clb). **199 Becca Cahall:** (t). **200-201 Becca Cahall:** (bl). **202 Becca Cahall:** (t). **203 Becca Cahall:** (b). **204 Shutterstock.com:** Craig Waltrip (b). **205 Becca Cahall:** (br). **206 Alamy Stock Photo:** Cavan Images / Aurora Open RF / Corey Rich (tl). **207 Getty Images / iStock:** E+ / PamelaJoeMcFarlane (t). **209 Getty Images:** Moment / Ruben Earth. **210-211 Alamy Stock Photo:** Bill Gozansky. **212 Matty Van Biene:** (t). **213 Matty Van Biene:** (tr). **214 Matty Van Biene:** (l). **216 Matty Van Biene:** (t)

Cover images: *Front and Back:* **Shutterstock.com:** Dancake (background); *Front:* **Ken Etzel**; *Back:* **Matty Van Biene:** tr; **Bobby Biskupiak:** br; **Jason Hummel:** bc; **Nate Ptacek:** bl

All other images © Dorling Kindersley

Acknowledgements

By default, storytelling is the work of many. First, there are those who are brave enough to speak. The thoughtful listen. In between, there are those who sharpen emotion and laughter. While The Dirtbag Diaries started many years ago as a single voice coming from a makeshift sound booth in a tiny closet, it almost immediately evolved into a community endeavor. To witness and help our outdoor community grow, evolve, find its voice, and strive has been the joy of my career. While I have been the one to adapt this show into print, these stories are the work of many.

None of this is possible without you, the outdoor community. Thanks to everyone who has ever submitted a Short, sent us a story idea, or introduced us to someone you felt that we needed to know. The growth and reach of this project is a reflection of your excitement about it. When the technology was lacking, you downloaded episodes to iPods or burned it to CDs to share with friends. In the era of social sharing, you championed us on platforms and talked us up around campfires. With no marketing budget or public relationships campaigns, you grew us and that growth led to more stories and more voices. This project is ultimately a reflection of you.

Through the years, three incredible producers have left an indelible mark on the Diaries. Thank you Jen Altschul for having the drive, vision, and follow through that allowed us to punch above our weight. You blazed the way in a critical moment. Cordelia Zars brought an emotional intelligence, an endurance athlete's stamina, and a musician's sense of timing and impact. You carried the Diaries through the pandemic years when the show was a critical connection point as our community processed the world's events. Lauren Delaunay Miller brought a mountain of energy, a blizzard of ideas, and a lifetime's worth of her own crazy stories, experiences, and hijinx. We look forward to the coming years.

Through his illustrations, my brother Walker Cahall continues to crystallize the stories onto the page. It's a deep joy to see you play in your creative sandbox. Through her work at our parent company Duct Tape Then Beer, Anya Miller was a true champion of the show and brought her creative superpowers, zest for life and deep love of community to the campfire. Your creative talents still hover over the show. Leici Hendrix has stood shoulder to shoulder alongside Becca and I as we navigated the business of creativity. We both deeply appreciate your wisdom and friendship. Ashlee Langholz, thank you for your always steadying presence and for keeping us moving forward.

Patagonia was there for the Diaries from the beginning before most companies even knew there was such a thing as podcast advertising. Special thanks to Kasey Kersnowski, Whitney Connor-Clapper, Alison Huyett, Scott Carrington, and Audrey Sherman for helping tell impactful stories. Kuat Racks has also been unwavering in its support. Thank you Luke Kuschmeader and Kristy Taylor. Ride on.

Thank you so much to the team at DK for coming to us with a vision for this book. Flo Ward and Pete Jorgensen, your enthusiasm for these stories was a gift. As someone who perpetually looks forward and struggles to acknowledge successes, this was a moment to feel gratitude for this project, our team, and our community. Thank you to Tom Howells for bearing with me as I remembered how to write for print and to Millie Acers for your tenacity in reaching out to people who prefer to be off the grid. Thank you to Eoghan O'Brien and Isabelle Merry for the design vision and to all the photographers whose images sparkle—you've made these stories come to life on the page.

To my boys Teplin and Wiley, thank you for being willing collaborators in this creative experiment. I know there are only the fuzziest of boundaries between what I consider life and work, and you show great patience and curiosity. Please keep showing me the way.

Most of all to Becca. None of this happens without you. People often ask if it's difficult to have your creative collaborator be your life partner. I stare at them blankly because it's hard for me to imagine an existence without the life we've created together. I love you as big as the world.

Editors Flo Ward, Millie Acers
Designers Eoghan O'Brien, Isabelle Merry
Senior Acquisitions Editor Pete Jorgensen
Design Manager Jo Connor
Production Editor Jen Murray
Production Controller Louise Daly

DK would like to thank Caroline West for proofreading
and Madeline Gee for indexing.

First American Edition, 2024
Published in the United States by DK Publishing
1450 Broadway, Suite 801, New York, NY 10018

Page design copyright © 2024 Dorling Kindersley Limited
DK, a Division of Penguin Random House LLC
24 25 26 27 28 10 9 8 7 6 5 4 3 2 1
001–338961–Jun/2024

The authorised representative in the EEA is
Dorling Kindersley Verlag GmbH. Arnulfstr. 124,
80636 Munich, Germany

Published in Great Britain by Dorling Kindersley Limited

A catalog record for this book
is available from the Library of Congress.
ISBN 978-0-7440-9271-4

DK books are available at special discounts
when purchased in bulk for sales promotions, premiums, fund-
raising, or educational use. For details, contact: DK Publishing
Special Markets, 1450 Broadway, Suite 801, New York, NY
10018
SpecialSales@dk.com

www.dk.com

MIX
Paper | Supporting
responsible forestry
FSC™ C018179

This book was made with Forest
Stewardship Council™ certified
paper – one small step in DK's
commitment to a sustainable future.
**Learn more at www.dk.com/uk/
information/sustainability**